Through the Year with Mary

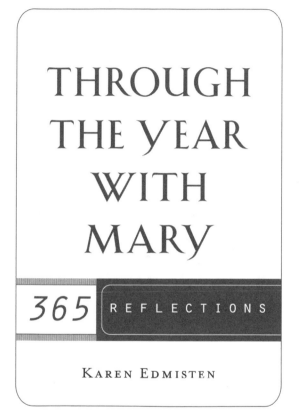

THROUGH
THE YEAR
WITH
MARY

365 REFLECTIONS

KAREN EDMISTEN

SERVANT
BOOKS

PUBLISHED BY ST. ANTHONY MESSENGER PRESS
CINCINNATI, OHIO

:   *For Jack, of course*   :

Scripture passages have been taken from the *Revised Standard Version*, Catholic edition.
Copyright 1946, 1952, 1971 by the Division of Christian Education of the National Council
of Churches of Christ in the USA. Used by permission. All rights reserved.

Quotes are taken from the English translation of the *Catechism of the Catholic Church* for the
United States of America, 2nd ed. Copyright 1997 by United States Catholic Conference—
Libreria Editrice Vaticana.

Cover and book design by Mark Sullivan
Cover photo copyright © Stockbyte | Punchstock.com

LIBRARY OF CONGRESS CATALOGING-IN-PUBLICATION DATA
Edmisten, Karen.
Through the year with Mary : 365 meditations / Karen Edmisten.
p. cm.
Includes bibliographical references and index.
ISBN 978-0-86716-937-9 (pbk. : alk. paper) 1. Mary, Blessed Virgin, Saint—Prayers and
devotions. 2. Devotional calendars—Catholic Church. 3. Catholic Church—Prayers and
devotions. I. Title.
BX2160.23.E34 2010
242'.2—dc22
                                        2010026536
ISBN 978-0-86716-937-9

Published by Servant Books, an imprint of St. Anthony Messenger Press.
28 W. Liberty St.
Cincinnati, OH 45202
www.AmericanCatholic.org
www.ServantBooks.org

Printed in the United States of America.
Printed on acid-free paper.

10 11 12 13 14 5 4 3 2 1

C O N T E N T S

: *A C K N O W L E D G M E N T S* :

Colossal thanks to the following, who shared favorite quotes, lent me books, suggested sources, offered ideas, spirited my children away for a day, or encouraged me to have another cup of coffee: Cynthia Cavnar, Tom, Emily, Lizzy, and Kate Edmisten, Jack Donnelly, Libby Donnelly, Fr. Joe Taphorn, Andrea Schlickbernd, Jennifer McGonigle, Bridget O'Brien, Johnna Miller, Danae Henkel, Fr. Scott Hastings, Donna-Marie Cooper O'Boyle, María Ruiz Scaperlanda, Lissa Peterson, Alicia Van Hecke, and my online network of writing pals. Thank you to Lucy Scholand for her excellent editor's eye. And special gratitude goes out to Suzie Andres for the gift that arrived on the Feast of Our Lady of the Rosary.

I didn't think I was the type.

People who had a Marian devotion were...well, they weren't me.

I converted to Catholicism after years of atheism, and although I had questions about Mary ("Whoa! Where'd that Assumption stuff come from?" and "Queen of everything? Really?"), Marian doctrines weren't my greatest stumbling block. I found satisfying explanations, and once I accepted the teaching authority of the Church, I filed those explanations under "The magisterium knows better than I."

So "the Mary question" was intellectually settled for me. But I did dive into Catholic waters still slightly uncomfortable with that "Blessed Mother" title. Soon I was drowning in titles: Our Lady, Blessed Virgin Mary, Mystical Rose, Ark of the Covenant, Cause of Our Joy..."Honestly," I thought, "how many names does one woman need?"

I recall the first time I used one of those names out loud. I was helping with RCIA, and I tentatively referred to "ummm, the Blessed Mother..." with the same hesitation a child might use when trying out a sophisticated new word. It felt—how can I explain it?—different but not bad, not wrong or pretentious. Just new.

As I began to employ the vocabulary peculiar to Catholicism, I realized that I was beginning to think a little differently about Mary too. She was blessed—a mother blessed in a way I couldn't fully comprehend and hadn't, in many ways, ever considered.

That shift in thinking is what words can do for us. They help us see things anew, conjure fresh images, give voice to our unspoken longings, and express what we feel about the people we hold dear.

It was in paying closer attention to words that my relationship with Mary grew. Relationships require give and take. Before I started paying attention, I had only taken from Mary. I took facts—the knowledge that she was there, that she was available, that she was the mother of Jesus—and I filed those facts about Mary away. Most of all I took her for granted.

But when I accepted the idea of a relationship, I found that things started happening. I'd pray a Hail Mary and see a minor shift in a situation I prayed for. Or I'd offer a rosary for an impossible intention and see a startling result. I'd have a glimmer of hope that a woman in heaven was really listening to me.

When I became a mother for the second time, about a year after I came into the Church, I found myself pondering Mary's early days of motherhood. I later lost a baby, and in my pain I sympathized with Mary, who had to watch her Son suffer and die. I asked her to sympathize with me too. I knew she understood my grief.

Imperceptibly something grew. I realized one day that without even thinking about it, that I often turned to Mary to ask her prayers. I found in her a model for me in every way: as a daughter, a woman, a wife, a mother, a friend, a disciple. She was one who experienced loss, who dutifully carried out every responsibility, who said yes to God again and again, even when God's requests were shocking or seemed dreadful.

She was everything she was created to be. And she showed me what I could be.

And that's what this collection of words is about: looking at Mary—and at ourselves—in a new way, opening up to the possibility that a fresh turn of phrase can sharpen our vision and bring something into focus, something that might have been fuzzy all our lives. I hope just a few words about Mary every day—exquisite quotes from people much wiser than I, and my own brief thoughts about those quotes—will draw us closer to Mary and, in the process, draw us closer to Jesus, which is where Mary wants us.

It's about a relationship—with a mother, the Blessed Mother, our mother. Because Mary doesn't have a type. She's here for all of us, every day.

January 1 | Solemnity of Mary, Mother of God

What can I wish for you but that you will always listen to these words of Mary, the Mother of Christ: "Do whatever he tells you"? And may you accept those words with your hearts, because they were uttered from the heart. From the heart of Mother.

—POPE JOHN PAUL II

Mary, may the words of your heart become my words, so that I will do whatever he tells me.

January 2

Mary is special, in that she alone was chosen by God to be the "ark of the covenant" by which God entered fully into our world....

On the other hand, Mary is really more normal than any of us, if by "normal" we mean closer to what God originally intended human beings to be.

—ALAN SCHRECK

Father, let me strive to be what you intended—to be as extraordinarily "normal" as our Blessed Mother was.

January 3

Mary's single word is all we need to know. All the secret of sanctity is here: "Be it done to me according to Thy word." For "Thy word" has been revealed as Jesus.

—PETER KREEFT

Lord, help me hear your word today and say yes.

January 4

I do not want to be in a religion in which I am *allowed* to have a crucifix. I feel the same about the much more controversial question of the honor paid to the blessed Virgin. If people do not like that cult, they are quite right not to be Catholics. But in people who are Catholics, or call themselves Catholics, I want the idea not only liked but loved and loved ardently, and above all proudly proclaimed.

—G.K. CHESTERTON

I can proudly proclaim my love for you, Mary, for you are a great and worthy guide.

January 5

Mary's role as mediatrix of miracles began at Cana. It has continued ever since. And its function is the same, so that his disciples might believe in him and obey him in all things.

—FR. JOHN HARDON, S.J.

May I always believe in and obey your Son in everything I do, Mary.

January 6

When they saw the star, they rejoiced exceedingly with great joy; and going into the house they saw the child with Mary his mother, and they fell down and worshiped him. Then, opening their treasures, they offered him gifts, gold and frankincense and myrrh.

—GOSPEL OF MATTHEW 2:10–11

God, grant me the eyes to see, the ears to hear, and the heart to grasp your epiphanies in my life.

January 7

Mother! Call her with a loud voice. She is listening to you; she sees you in danger, perhaps, and she—your holy mother Mary—offers you, along with the grace of her son, the refuge of her arms, the tenderness of her embrace,...and you will find yourself with added strength for the new battle.

—St. Josemaría Escrivá

Thank you, Mother, for your love, which strengthens me
daily for the battle of life.

January 8 | Feast of Our Lady of Prompt Succor

In dangers, in doubts, in difficulties, think of Mary, call upon Mary. Let not her name leave your lips, never suffer it to leave your heart.

—St. Bernard of Clairvaux

Mary, be with me in all things today; be in my heart.

January 9

Mary has much to teach us about humility. She was full of grace, yet she was only the handmaid of the Lord. She was the Mother of God yet served as a handmaid in the house of Elizabeth. She was immaculately conceived yet she humbly met Jesus, himself humiliated, carrying his cross.

—Bl. Teresa of Calcutta

Lord, give me the grace of humility in all ways and things.

January 10

Advocate and Refuge of Sinners, Advocate of Penitents, Advocate of the Poor, Advocate of the Universal Church, Tender Advocate, Wise Advocate.

—TITLES OF THE BLESSED VIRGIN MARY

My advocate. Thank you, Mary, for hearing my prayers
and hastening them to your Son.

January 11

Mary…modeled for us three great secrets of spiritual power: pondering, positivity, and praise.

—PETER KREEFT

Simple actions and attitudes lead to powerful gifts of grace.

January 12

I force myself in vain to meditate on the mysteries of the rosary; I don't succeed in fixing my mind on them. For a long time I was desolate about this lack of devotion which astonished me, for I love the Blessed Virgin so much that it should be easy for me to recite in her honor prayers which are so pleasing to her. Now I am less desolate; I think that the Queen of heaven, since she is my Mother, must see my good will and she is satisfied with it.

—ST. THÉRÈSE OF LISIEUX

A great saint admitted her struggles with prayer; pray for me to humbly persevere,
Mary, just as the Little Flower did.

January 13

She carries her child as every mother carries her first child, and yet in spirit she must be prepared for the carrying of the sin of the world through her son.

—ADRIENNE VON SPEYR

Great gifts can bring great crosses and responsibilities. Help me, Lord, to accept the crosses with faith and to carry them with trust.

January 14

Mother, dear, lend me your heart. I look for it each day to pour my troubles into.

—ST. GEMMA GALGANI

Mary, you listen to me with a mother's heart;
your prayers are a salve for my troubled soul.

January 15

I always say to the Blessed Mother after Communion—"Here He is in my heart; I believe, help thou my unbelief; Adore Him, thank Him and love Him for me. He is your Son; His honor is in your hands. Do not let me dishonor Him."

—DOROTHY DAY

Mary, my connection to you is also my connection to Jesus.
Pray for me to love and honor him as you did.

January 16

The child does not enter the world apart from Mary his blessed mother, the theotokos. In her pilgrimage of faith, hope, and love she blazes the trail on which the Church is to follow.

—CARDINAL AVERY DULLES, S.J.

In following God's plan Mary became a leader to us all,
showing the way of a true disciple.

January 17

The first thing which kindles ardor in learning is the greatness of the teacher. What is greater than the Mother of God? What more glorious than she whom Glory Itself chose?

—St. Ambrose

To learn from Mary is to learn from a handpicked spiritual master.

January 18

Our good Jesus and His most blessed Mother are too good company to be left and He is well pleased if we grieve at His pains, even though sometimes at the cost of our own consolations and joys.

—St. Teresa of Avila

Keeping company with Jesus and Mary is not always easy. But it is always the best.

January 19

One must accept the call, one must listen, one must receive, one must measure one's strength, and answer, "Yes, yes." Fear not, fear not because you have found grace, do not fear life, do not fear your maternity, do not fear your marriage, do not fear your priesthood, for you have found grace. This certainty, this consciousness, helps us as it helped Mary.

—Pope John Paul II

You have called me to this life, Lord. Thank you, Papa and Blessed Mother, for reminding me: "Be not afraid!"

January 20

Men do not fear a powerful hostile army as the powers of hell fear the name and protection of Mary.

—St. Bonaventure

Darkness has no power over me when I call on the Mother of my Lord.

January 21

She was a reed through which the Eternal Love was to be piped as a shepherd's song.

—CARYLL HOUSELANDER

May I, too, be an instrument in the hands of the Lord.

January 22

She is the Queen longing for us to be part of the heavenly kingdom, the Mother longing to enfold all her children within the mantle of her love, especially those who have wandered far from home.

—FR. JOHN LOCHRAN

I'll pray today for lost souls, prodigal sons, strangers, and sojourners.
Mary longs for their return.

January 23

God, in his mercy, does not tell us everything our yes will mean. Most likely, Mary did not understand everything her yes would mean. She had much to ponder; however, she still gave God permission to work in and through her life as he saw fit. Like Mary, we don't have to know everything our yes will mean; we just have to yield ourselves, trusting God.

—KIMBERLY HAHN

Lord, let me say yes without counting the cost.
Then help me to bear the cost for your sake.

January 24

Indeed full of grace, for to others it is given in portions, but on Mary its fullness is showered.

—ST. JEROME

When I use the portion of grace I've been given, I cooperate with God and his plan.

January 25

Sooner would heaven and earth perish, than would she deprive of her help any one earnestly imploring her aid. Give thanks to the Lord, who has given her to thee for a Mother and a helper.

—ABBOT LOUIS OF BLOIS

Thank you, Lord, for this most precious and eager mother, helper, and intercessor.

January 26

Oh! How happy are the souls who, in imitation of this holy Virgin, consecrate themselves to the service of God from their childhood.... They are like beautiful flowers freshly blown, that have not been touched or withered by the heat of concupiscence, spreading around, by their virtues and their purity, an odor of great sweetness before God.

—ST. FRANCIS DE SALES

Holy Virgin, help me to imitate you and spread the sweetness of God.

January 27

The song Mary sings is called a victory song precisely because her life shows the personal and universal love of God on a grand scale. God achieves victory through Mary's submission to his freedom and by her willing embrace of his plan.

—FR. GARY CASTER

I too am a part of both God's personal and his universal love.
May I willingly embrace that knowledge and act on God's plan for me.

January 28

The New Testament is filled with evidence of the power and efficacy of the holy name of Jesus.... Happy are they who can imitate the blessed Mary in her relation to this holy name, who conceive it in their hearts by salutary desires, give birth to it in works of virtue, and persevere in invoking it to the end of their lives.

—St. Robert Bellarmine

Do I imitate Mary regarding the Holy Name of Jesus?
Do I speak of him with reverence, awe, and love?

January 29

Consider the heroic faith of Mary in those dark moments on Good Friday. Gabriel originally told her that she would be the mother of Israel's Messiah, the mother of the One whose kingdom would have no end. Yet as John Paul II points out, at the foot of the cross Mary would be a witness, from a human perspective, to the complete negation of those words about Christ's everlasting kingship....

How great then must have been her trust as she entered what could be called a "spiritual crucifixion," letting go of her son and abandoning herself to God's care in this time of darkness.

—Edward Sri

Father, sometimes my expectation of your work in my life seems completely negated by circumstances. I aspire to the kind of trust Mary placed in you.
Help me to accept my own spiritual crucifixions.

January 30

The fact that Mary progressed from daughter to wife and from mother to widow gives us much to appreciate about her pilgrimage of faith. She offers an example of holiness in so many vocations that all women can find common ground with at least a portion of her life on earth. Like all of us, she stepped out in faith, unsure of where her path would lead but fully confident in the plan of God yet to be revealed.

—GENEVIEVE KINEKE

Daughter, wife, mother, widow—Mary is a model for every woman.
In her trusting faith she is a model for all people.

January 31

Eve, the Mother of All the Living, long ago became the Mother of All the Dying by her disobedience. Similarly, on Mary's obedience, as on Eve's disobedience, hung the fate of our race. In saying yes to God, Mary was not a tool but a person; not a robot but "God's fellow worker" (1 Cor 3:9).

—MARK SHEA

I must always remember that God gave Mary a choice;
she did not have to say yes. But she did.

February 1

Blessed Mother Teresa of Calcutta, who was very dear to Pope John Paul II, told me on a number of occasions to call upon the Blessed Mother for help, strength, and safety. She taught me a simple but powerful prayer, "Mary, Mother of Jesus, be a Mother to me now."

—Donna-Marie Cooper O'Boyle

Call on Mary—always! A mother's help is never far away.

February 2 | Feast of the Presentation of the Lord

"Lord, now let your servant depart in peace,
according to your word;
for my eyes have seen your salvation
which you have prepared in the presence of all peoples,
a light for revelation to the Gentiles,
and for glory to your people Israel."

And his father and his mother marveled at what was said about him.

—Gospel of Luke 2:29–33

Like Mary, I marvel at our Savior. May I always recognize him as Simeon did.

February 3

It's good to speak of [Mary's] privileges, but it's necessary above all that we can imitate her. She prefers imitation to admiration and her life was so simple.... How I like singing to her: The narrow road to heaven you have made visible...when practicing always the most humble virtues.

—St. Thérèse of Lisieux

Mary, what one thing can I do today that is in imitation of you?

February 4

The Word could have incarnated himself without being born of a woman, but he wished to take on flesh in Mary so as to really enter into human history, so as to possess a genealogy as do all other men, so as to belong in truth to our race. Thanks to the Virgin Mary, Jesus is not only like us because he is a man but he is one of us, capable of representing us before the Father in virtue of bonds of blood; and in exchange he can communicate his divine life to us because of his organic connection with the mass of humanity.

—Fr. Jacques Bur

Lord, you chose to come to us through a woman, and in doing so you gave all of humanity a new dignity and beauty.

February 5

Most blessed Star of the Sea, dispel the storms besetting me.
Most virtuous, holy and sweet, guide me on the way.

—St. Robert Bellarmine

Mary, calm and steady, stay with me through any storm I encounter today.

February 6

Mary is the heart of the church. This is why all works of charity spring from her. It is well known that the heart has two movements: systole and diastole. Thus Mary is always performing these two movements: absorbing grace from her Most Holy Son, and pouring it forth on sinners.

—St. Anthony Mary Claret

Mary, you keep me intimately connected to Jesus.

February 7

Keep my heart close to yours, Mother—you make me whole, and I will love you forever.

—Immaculée Ilibagiza

Mary, you inspire in me a childlike love and affection,
reminding me that I am safe in your care.

February 8

The spikenard is a little shrub which never raises itself aloft.... We may, indeed, say with truth that the Blessed Virgin is like very precious spikenard, for she never exalted herself on account of all the great graces and favors which she received, or the praises which were given to her, but always remained beautiful in her lowliness and her littleness.

—St. Francis de Sales

I make proper use of my gifts when I remember that they came from the Lord. They are
his and are meant to be used for his glory.

February 9

Let us, my daughters, in some small degree, imitate the great humility of the most sacred Virgin, whose habit we wear and whose nuns we are ashamed to call ourselves.... I say "in some degree" because, however much we may seem to humble ourselves, we fall far short of being the daughters of such a Mother, and the brides of such a Spouse.

—St. Teresa of Avila

I have so very far to go, Mother Mary. Pray for me.

February 10

When my daughter was born almost eighteen years ago, I turned her over to the Blessed Mother. "What kind of a mother am I going to be?" I kept thinking to myself. "What kind of a Catholic home is she going to have, with only me?"...

There was a solution, of course, to such a difficulty. "You," I told the Blessed Mother, "will have to be her mother."

—Dorothy Day

Mary, you help me fill in the missing pieces of my life.

February 11 | Feast of Our Lady of Lourdes

How glad was my soul, O good Mother,
when I had the grace to look upon you!
How I love to recall those sweet moments
when I was beheld in eyes so full of kindness and mercy....
Yes, gentle Mother, you stooped down to earth
to appear to a mere child and, in spite of her unworthiness,
to communicate certain things to her.
You, the Queen of heaven and earth, wanted to make use of the most
fragile thing in the eyes of the world.

—St. Bernadette Soubirous

Make use of my frailties, good Mother, for your Son's glory.

February 12

Comfort of Christians, Comfort of Mourners, Consolation of the Human Race, My Comfort, Sure and True, Our Consolation in the Hour of Death, Solace of Our Pilgrimage, Solace of the Wretched, Tender Comforter.

—TITLES OF THE BLESSED VIRGIN MARY

Mary, your maternal consolation will see me through every challenge.

February 13

There is no sense of the power of God that could produce the Incarnation and the Resurrection. They [the public] are all so busy explaining away the virgin birth and such things, reducing everything to human proportions that in time they lose even the sense of the human itself, what they were aiming to reduce everything to.

—FLANNERY O'CONNOR

Lord, through the Blessed Virgin Mary, you transformed "human proportions." Help me carry that message of hope to someone who needs to hear it.

February 14

"Do whatever he tells you." That is Mary's message to us, as well as to the servants at the wedding feast in Cana. "Do whatever he tells you" is Mary's gentle invitation to make her fiat your own. Don't look for an "exit strategy." Live in trust, not in calculation; stake everything on Christ.

—GEORGE WEIGEL

I accept your invitation, Mother Mary, to say yes and live in trust.

February 15

Who is this virgin so worthy of reverence as to be saluted by an angel: yet so humble as to be betrothed to a carpenter?

—St. Bernard of Clairvaux

Who are you, Mary? A servant and a queen, both humble and holy.
In your smallness I see your greatness.

February 16

If you are in danger, she will hasten to free you. If you are troubled, she will console you. If you are sick, she will bring you relief. If you are in need, she will help you. She does not look to see what kind of a person you have been. She simply comes to a heart that wants to love her.

—St. Gabriel Possenti

Mary, help of sinners and font of mercy, pray for me.

February 17

After the knowledge of God had been universally lost or obscured, one man from the whole earth (Abraham) is picked out. He is separated (miserably enough, we may suppose) from his natural surroundings, sent into a strange country, and made the ancestor of a nation who are to carry the knowledge of the true God. Within this nation there is further selection: some die in the desert, some remain behind in Babylon.... The process grows narrower and narrower, sharpens at last into one small bright point like the head of a spear. It is a Jewish girl at her prayers. All humanity (so far as concerns its redemption) has narrowed to that.

—C.S. Lewis

May I never forget the work of God accomplished through a single,
humble soul named Mary.

February 18

I cannot promise you the happiness of this world but of the other.

—THE BLESSED VIRGIN MARY, TO ST. BERNADETTE
SOUBIROUS AT LOURDES, FRANCE

Lord, I offer up any distress and unhappiness I experience today
for the conversion of sinners.

February 19

See in her the pattern of your life, for in her, as though in a model, manifest teachings of goodness show what you should correct, what you should copy and what preserve.... For such was Mary that her life alone suffices for the instruction of all.

—ST. AMBROSE

I want to imitate Mary by being open to Christ, following Christ,
leading others to Christ and his love.

February 20

She seeks for those who approach her devoutly and with reverence, for such she loves, nourishes, and adopts as her children.

—ST. BONAVENTURE

I'm an unworthy child, Mother Mary; thank you for adopting me as your own.

February 21

I think, if I had understood then, as I do now, how this great King really dwells within this little palace of my soul, I should not have left Him alone so often.... How wonderful it is that He Whose greatness could fill a thousand worlds, and very many more, should confine Himself within so small a space, just as He was pleased to dwell within the womb of His most holy Mother!

—ST. TERESA OF AVILA

Jesus dwelling within me: The reality is hard to grasp.
Mary, be my example of surrender.

February 22

Our Lady said yes for the human race. Each one of us must echo that yes for our own lives.

We are all asked if we will surrender what we are…and allow Christ to fill the emptiness formed by the particular shape of our life.

The surrender that is asked of us includes complete and absolute trust; it must be like Our Lady's surrender, without condition and without reservation.

—CARYLL HOUSELANDER

*When I struggle to understand how God is working in my life, may I have the grace
to keep trusting, to give my permission again and again.*

February 23

I must keep watch if I am not to lose purity; in my temptations… I shall have recourse to Mary who is purity itself.

—ST. CATHERINE LABOURÉ

*Mary, guide me daily in the virtues of modesty, purity,
and chastity within my station in life.*

February 24

It could be said that from the very beginning there was a Christological focus in Christianity.

…A remarkable expression of it is found in Marian devotion and in Mariology: "He was conceived by the Holy Spirit and born of the Virgin Mary" (Apostles' Creed). A Marian dimension and Mariology in the Church are simply another aspect of the Christological focus.

—POPE JOHN PAUL II

To look to Mary is to see her source: Jesus.

February 25

If we would completely rejoice the heart of God, let us strive in all things to conform ourselves to his divine will.... To this end we should always invoke the aid of our holy patrons, our guardian angels, and above all, of our mother Mary, the most perfect of all the saints because she most perfectly embraced the divine will.

—St. Alphonsus de Liguori

Have I called on my patrons, my guardian angel, and my mother Mary today?

February 26

Mary recognizes that just as the heavens and the earth wordlessly proclaim the greatness of God, so also does her life. Her soul has become a lens through which others might better see God and his divine mystery. Mary's life is an instrument through which the world can see more clearly the Love that God is.

—Fr. Gary Caster

*Let my life be a clear lens too—crystalline clean and pure—
so that the Lord can shine through.*

February 27

No sooner had Mary consented to be Mother of the eternal Word, than she merited by this consent to be made Queen of the world and of all creatures.

—St. Bernardine of Siena

Mary was free to consent or decline. What is God asking of me today?

February 28

The love of our Mother will be the breath that kindles into a living flame the embers of virtue that are hidden under the ashes of your indifference.

—St. Josemaría Escrivá

Lord, I am so sorry for the times I've been indifferent.
Mary, pray for me to be—and to remain—on fire.

March 1

We take refuge under the protection of your motherly mercy, O Mother of God. Despise not our fervent cries for help in the necessity in which we find ourselves. But deliver us from danger. Rescue us. Do not lead our plea into temptation, but deliver us from danger.

—EARLY CHRISTIAN TEXT

Mary, mother of mercy, protect me today from all physical and spiritual danger.
Armed with your intercession, I can face anything.

March 2

Being a wife and mother was never an obstacle to my spiritual life.

—CONCEPCION CABRERA DE ARMIDA

Mary, you were the greatest of all mystics, yet you lived a simple vocation.
May I live my vocation as faithfully and as well.

March 3

Beloved and Chosen Daughter, Daughter of Saints Joachim and Anne, Daughter of the Light Eternal, Daughter of the Sovereign King, Illustrious Daughter of the House of David, Most Obedient Daughter, Most Pure Daughter.

—TITLES OF THE BLESSED VIRGIN MARY

Mary—perfect virgin, perfect wife, perfect mother, perfect daughter—
you show me beauty in every role you play.

March 4

When a room is heated by an open fire, surely there is nothing strange in the fact that those who stand closest to the fireplace are the ones who are warmest. And when God comes into the world through the instrumentality of one of His servants, then there is nothing surprising about the fact that His chosen instrument should have the greatest and most intimate share in the divine gift.

—Fr. Thomas Merton

May I be warmed by the fire of the one closest to Jesus—Mary, my mother.

March 5

My Immaculate Queen of heaven and earth, refuge of sinners and Mother most loving; you to whom God entrusted the entire order of mercy. I am an unworthy sinner. I cast myself at your feet, humbly pleading that you ordain to accept me completely and totally as your property and possession and do with me, and all my powers of body and soul, and with all my life and death and eternity, whatever is pleasing to you.

—St. Maximilian Kolbe

Today I'll remember the motto of Pope John Paul II, Totus Tuus!
I am totally yours, Mary.

March 6

He who is devout to the Virgin Mother will certainly never be lost.

—St. Ignatius of Antioch

Devotion to Mary is devotion to our Lord. Mary, you will never lead me astray.

March 7

Imagine Mary, a young girl at her prayers or perhaps performing her tasks or simply sitting and watching people pass by her window. Suddenly, there is a rush of wind like a flutter of wings, or a flash of light, and there is one like an angel addressing her....

All mystics wonder what is happening to them when the Holy Spirit asks them to believe the seemingly impossible, that God wants to enter their lives. They can, of course, refuse out of fear or doubt, and it is the glory of Mary that she does not refuse but says yes.

—Fr. Murray Bodo

Am I fearful? Do I lack understanding? Mary, help me say yes,
even when things seem incomprehensible or impossible.

March 8

She and Christ were so one in their love that the greatness of her love caused the greatness of her suffering.

—Julian of Norwich

May I unite my life and my suffering with that of Jesus, as faithfully as Mary did.

March 9

If some disturbance overtakes me, some embarrassment, I turn very quickly to her and as the most tender of Mothers she always takes care of my interests.

—St. Thérèse of Lisieux

Mary, help me remember that nothing is too trivial for or beyond the reach
of your prayers.

March 10

A new Adam—Jesus—would reign, as had been foreshadowed in the garden and in the courts of Solomon. The New Adam, the new Davidic monarch, would reign with His bride, the New Eve, and she would be a real historical woman, whom Revelation would identify with the Church. She would be mother of the living. She would be advocate of the people. She would be queen mother. She would be Mary.

—SCOTT HAHN

Thank you, Lord, for the gift of Mary—my advocate, my queen, my mother.

March 11

When a fire is kindled and many logs surround it, the log most apt and efficient for combustion will be the quickest to catch the flame and burn. So it was with Mary. For when the fire of divine love—which in itself is changeless and eternal—began to kindle and appear, and when the Godhead willed to become incarnate, no creature was more apt and efficient for receiving this fire of love than the Virgin Mary; for no creature burned with such charity as she.

—ST. BRIDGET OF SWEDEN

Mary, pray for me, that I will always burn with love for God.

March 12

Perhaps you have even pondered upon how Mary felt as she bore Jesus in her womb: You too can experience that same privilege when you have Jesus living within you after Communion.

—FR. JOHN H. HAMPSCH, C.M.F.

What a miracle and a privilege! Though Mary carried Jesus within her in a unique way, I have been given an intimate relationship with him too.

March 13

Our Lady intercedes in favor of life, not one life, but the life of the whole of humanity. She is there with us in times of temptation to crush the "head of the serpent." She is there in our times of difficulty when "the wine has run out." She stands at the foot of our every cross, praying and waiting for us to rise again.

—Fr. John Lochran

Thank you, Mary, for walking next to me on every step of this journey.

March 14

And whenever anyone had a need, the cry resounded, "Take it to the queen!" for the king, cherishing his spouse's virtues, and recognizing his own will and likeness in her, could refuse her no request.

—Josephine Nobisso

Take every petition to our queen; she is waiting to help and pray.

March 15

It would be strange if the Queen of Mothers, whose glory consists precisely in giving and blessing, should refuse her aid to those whom she has brought forth spiritually.

—St. Just de Bretenières

A good mother will not refuse to help her children, and Mary is the best of all mothers.

March 16

With (Mary) for guide, thou shalt never go astray; whilst invoking her, thou shalt never lose heart; so long as she is in thy mind, thou shalt not be deceived.

—St. Bernard of Clairvaux

Mary is the steady, guiding light who brings hope and peace in an unsteady world.

March 17

Like [Mary], great are the graces we have received. Like her, let us always accept the cross in whatever way it comes. Like her, let us with grace and delicacy touch the lonely and unwanted. Like her, let us not be ashamed or slow to do humble works.

—Bl. Teresa of Calcutta

The Mother of God washed dishes, changed diapers, and swept floors.
My daily work is often as mundane—and as holy.

March 18

More blessed was Mary in receiving Christ's faith than in conceiving Christ's flesh.

—St. Augustine

I cannot conceive Christ's flesh, but I consume it,
and in doing so I, too, receive his faith.

March 19

There are spiritual souls outside the Church which find it unbearable that a woman should be mother of God: for many such the way of escape is to speak of her as mother of the human nature of Christ. But natures do not have mothers. He who was born of her as man was God the Son. She was as totally his mother as yours is yours or mine mine.

—F.J. Sheed

Mary, Mother of God, singularly blessed, pray for the broken body of Christ.

March 20

Mary's world radically changes when the angel Gabriel appears to her saying, "Hail, full of grace, the Lord is with you!" Understandably, Mary "was greatly troubled."

—EDWARD SRI

In spite of being "greatly troubled," Mary trusted and was patient. Grant me the virtues of trust and patience today, Lord.

March 21

All of a sudden the Blessed Virgin appeared beautiful to me, so beautiful that I had never seen anything so attractive..... What penetrated to the very depths of my soul was the "ravishing smile of the Blessed Virgin."

—ST. THÉRÈSE OF LISIEUX

Smile on me today, Blessed Mother, and let me see the beauty of your soul.

March 22

O Mary, my queen and my mother, remember I am all yours. Keep me and guard me as your property and possession.

—ST. LOUIS DE MONTFORT

I am totally yours, Mary, and I'm at your disposal, to carry out the will of your Son.

March 23

It is especially consoling to note—and also accurate in accordance with the Gospel and history—that at the side of Christ, in the first and most exalted place, there is always His Mother through the exemplary testimony that she bears by her whole life to this particular Gospel of suffering. In her, the many and intense sufferings were amassed in such an interconnected way that they were not only a proof of her unshakeable faith but also a contribution to the Redemption of all.

—POPE JOHN PAUL II

Make my whole life a witness, Lord, to your work.

March 24

Notice how Gabriel greeted Mary: "Hail, full of grace, the Lord is with you!" He showed Mary deference, as though he, the angel— archangel, in fact, if you want to pull rank—was in awe of a humble Jewish woman who was hardly more than a girl. You'd think he was talking to somebody important.

—MIKE AQUILINA

Mary, Full of Grace, I stand in awe of you.

March 25 | Feast of the Annunciation

Behold, I am the handmaid of the Lord; let it be to me according to your word.

—MARY, GOSPEL OF LUKE 1:38

Total abandonment! You ask nothing less, Lord, and
I want to give you nothing less than this.

March 26

O Mother blest! And chosen shrine wherein the Architect divine
Whose hand contains the earth and sky vouchsafed in hidden guise
    to lie;
Blest in the message Gabriel brought; blest in the work the
    Spirit wrought;
Most blest, to bring to human birth the long desired of all the earth!

          —St. Venantius Fortunatus

Mary, so many have sung your praises throughout history.
I thank and praise you today too.

March 27

O Mary, my good Mother, may I follow your example
and be generous in all the sacrifices the Lord
will ask of me during the course of my life.

          —St. Bernadette Soubirous

Sometimes the sacrifices are painful. Help me, Mother Mary,
to call on you, and on all the saints, for help.

March 28

Go to the castle! Take our plight to the queen, who is, after all, one of
us! Ask her to beg the king's mercy.

          —Josephine Nobisso

Mary—one of us, and yet our queen. A staggering, beautiful, sublime truth.

March 29

My soul magnifies the Lord,
and my spirit rejoices in God my Savior....
For behold, henceforth all generations will call me blessed.

—Mary, Gospel of Luke 1:46–48

The Almighty One has done great things for me too.
May I rejoice today in his work in my life.

March 30

In [the words of the Magnificat] Mary's personal experience, the
ecstasy of her heart, shines forth. In them shines a ray of the mystery
of God, the glory of his ineffable holiness, the eternal love which, as an
irrevocable gift, enters into human history.

—Pope John Paul II

Lord, your work is beyond my grasp, and yet Mary reveals a glimpse
of your glory to me. My spirit rejoices.

March 31

Those wounds which were scattered over the body of our Lord were
all united in the single heart of Mary.

—St. Bonaventure

Immaculate Heart of Mary, a mother's heart, wounded for us.

April 1

Then he said to the disciple, "Behold, your mother!" And from that hour the disciple took her to his own home.

—GOSPEL OF JOHN 19:27

Jesus gave Mary to us as our mother. May I always honor his gift.

April 2

Him whom the heavens cannot contain, the womb of one woman bore. She ruled our Ruler; she carried Him in whom we are; she gave milk to our Bread.

—ST. AUGUSTINE

How weak my understanding is! How vast my gratitude!

April 3

Without her we would not have Jesus, we would not have our Brother, our Friend, our Savior. The loving abandonment of Mary is at the origin of our Redemption.

— FR. JEAN DU COEUR DE JÉSUS D'ELBÉE

If I abandon myself to you, Lord, what gifts can you bring to the world through my life?

April 4

No worship of Mary is more gracious than if you imitate Mary's humility.

—ERASMUS

Make me gracious. Humble me today, Lord.

April 5

Simeon blessed them and said to Mary his mother,

"Behold, this child is set for the fall and rising of many in Israel
and for a sign that is spoken against
(and a sword will pierce through your own soul also),
that thoughts out of many hearts may be revealed."

—GOSPEL OF LUKE 2:34–35

*Mary, your surrender to God's will brought great joy and unspeakable sorrow,
and yet you embraced it all. Help me to do likewise.*

April 6

Simeon's words seem like a second Annunciation to Mary, for they tell her of the actual historical situation in which the Son is to accomplish his mission, namely, in misunderstanding and sorrow. While this announcement on the one hand confirms her faith in the accomplishment of the divine promises of salvation, on the other hand it also reveals to her that she will have to live her obedience of faith in suffering, at the side of the suffering Savior, and that her motherhood will be mysterious and sorrowful.

—POPE JOHN PAUL II

*When my life seems to be all mystery and sorrow, help me, Lord, to recall
the courage of your Blessed Mother.*

April 7

What will be done in Mary is what God the Father wants for the human family: to experience the personal expression of his unconditional love. This is only possible because Mary trusts the Father enough to say, "Let it be to me according to your word."

—FR. GARY CASTER

*If I am to fully accept your love, Lord, I must have the strength to say, "Let it be to me
according to your word." Please give me that strength today.*

April 8

Beacon of Hope, Guide of Hope, Harbor of Refuge, Haven of the Tempest-Tossed, Help to the Helpless, Hope of All in Temptation, Hope of Christians, Hope of My Soul.

—TITLES OF THE BLESSED VIRGIN MARY

You never lost hope, dearest Mother, even at the most desperate time.
Be my hope, my haven, my help in all difficulties.

April 9

Men have crowded all her glory into a single phrase: the Mother of God. No one can say anything greater of her.

—MARTIN LUTHER

Lord, mend the divisions in your body by helping us all—Catholics and
non-Catholics alike—to give due honor to the Mother of God.

April 10

Far be it that anyone should try to defraud holy Mary of her privileges of divine grace and of her special glory. For by a certain singular favor of our Lord and God, and of her Son, she must be confessed to be the most true and most blessed Mother of God.

—ST. VINCENT OF LERINS

Holy Mary, Mother of God, chosen by God, your privileges and glory
draw me closer to your Son.

April 11

Show us your Christ, Lady, after this our exile, yes: but show Him to us also now, show Him to us here, while we are still wanderers.

—FR. THOMAS MERTON

Mary, help me, as I wander through this life of faith and doubt, to move
closer to your Son and to see him more clearly.

April 12

Mary's *fiat* to God illustrates a great truth about obedience: it brings new life.

—JOHNNETTE BENKOVIC

With obedience to God comes the greatest freedom imaginable.
Pray for me, Mary, to obey as faithfully as you did.

April 13

Mary attended to everything as though she were warned by many, and fulfilled every obligation of virtue as though she were teaching rather than learning.

—ST. AMBROSE

May I live my life this purposefully and well.

April 14

Have great confidence in the Holy Virgin; when we abandon ourselves to her it is impossible to go astray.

—ST. JUST DE BRETENIÈRES

Our Lord had complete confidence in Mary; shall I have any less?

April 15

For unless Our Lady is recognized as the Mother of God and as the Queen of all the saints and angels and as the hope of the world, faith in God will remain incomplete. How can we ask Him for all the things He would have us hope for if we do not know, by contemplating the sanctity of the Immaculate Virgin, what great things He has power to accomplish in the souls of men?

—FR. THOMAS MERTON

Hope of the world, God accomplished his greatest work in you. Let me cling with faith
to the knowledge that he will accomplish great things in my soul too.

April 16

I'm just a broom in the hands of the Virgin Mary.

—St. Bernadette Soubirous

Mary, use me for whatever work must be done.

April 17

So take heart and listen.
As God looked at Mary, as Mary looked at Bernadette,
So God looks at you with love.

—Fr. John Lochran

At its core the relationship is simple: God loves me; he wants me to love him.

April 18

We consecrate ourselves at one and the same time to the most holy Virgin and to Jesus Christ: to the most holy Virgin as to the perfect means that Jesus Christ Himself has chosen by which to unite Himself to us, and us to Him; and to our Lord as to our Last End, to whom as our Redeemer and our God, we owe all we are.

—St. Louis de Montfort

Mary, inseparable from Christ, lead me to him.

April 19

If a great dignitary, like a president or the pope, were to come and live in your home for a time, how carefully would you clean and prepare for that guest? If God planned to live for a time as a human being within the womb of a woman and then be taught and formed by this woman after his birth, how carefully would God prepare that woman for this awesome responsibility and privilege?

—Alan Schreck

The Immaculate Conception, while miraculous, is also simple common sense.
Thank you, Lord, for a faith with such reason.

April 20

A Virgin conceived, a Virgin bore, and a Virgin she remains.

—St. Peter Chrysologus

Mary, spouse of the Holy Spirit, may I accept and embrace the
things that are difficult to understand.

April 21

This then is what you must do, O Mary; since you love me, make me
like you. You have all power to change hearts; take then mine and
change it. Show the world what you can do for those who love you.
Make me a saint; make me your worthy child. This is my hope.

—St. Bonaventure

What must change in my heart? Mary, I'm yours; pray for my transformation.

April 22

Mary is the radiant sign and inviting model of the moral life.

—Pope John Paul II

An "inviting model"—Mary, your purity and beauty draw me
powerfully, irresistibly closer to God.

April 23

The truth like almost everything else relevant to membership in the
Mystical Body may best be studied in relation to Christ's mother,
because she is the one perfect member of the Body. Every element in
the life of the Body will be seen at its most intense in her.

—F.J. Sheed

Lord, help me as I imperfectly try to follow the perfect example set by Mary.

April 24

In the dark loneliness of the Passion, Our Lady offers her Son a comforting balm of tenderness, of union, of faithfulness; a "yes" to the divine will.

Hand in hand with Mary, you and I also want to console Jesus, by accepting always and in everything the will of His Father, of our Father.

Only thus will we taste the sweetness of Christ's cross and come to embrace it with all the strength of Love, carrying it in triumph along the ways of the earth.

—St. Josemaría Escrivá

May I always see in my sufferings a balm of tenderness,
a gift, a sacrifice to offer to my Lord.

April 25

Maryhouse [a residence for poor women], in effect, was [Dorothy] Day's response to the women's liberation movement. Maryhouse... was a community of women; it was a reminder that "the flesh of Jesus was the flesh of Mary," and a reminder of "how great the dignity of woman" is, "how large a part she played in the redemption of the world."

—Paul Elie

Both men and women are made in God's image. There's no need for a new movement
when the Lord has provided this original and authentic state of dignity.

April 26

God honored Mary by eternally predestining her to be the mother of the Savior—the one through whom God himself would enter into human history. What greater gift or dignity could God give to a human being? This honor given to Mary reveals the dignity of all women; a woman is more important in God's saving plan than any angel or other spiritual being.

—ALAN SCHRECK

The Lord loves and honors all women. Am I an evangelist of this beautiful message of grace and dignity?

April 27

O Lord God, my Creator and my Redeemer, I long to receive You this day with such reverence, praise, and honor, with such gratitude, worthiness and love, with such faith, hope, and purity as that with which Your most holy Mother, the glorious Virgin Mary, longed for and received You when she humbly and devoutly answered the angel who announced to her the mystery of the Incarnation.

—FR. THOMAS À KEMPIS

Mary, you excelled in every virtue. Pray for me, that I will always show every reverence to Christ, your Son, and will grow in virtue every day.

April 28

When the wine failed, the mother of Jesus said to him, "They have no wine." And Jesus said to her, "O woman, what have you to do with me? My hour has not yet come." His mother said to the servants, "Do whatever he tells you."

—GOSPEL OF JOHN 2:3–5

Daily I will endeavor to do this: whatever he tells me.

April 29

But while in the most holy Virgin the Church has already reached that perfection whereby she is without spot or wrinkle, the followers of Christ still strive to increase in holiness by conquering sin [see Ephesians 5:27]. And so they turn their eyes to Mary who shines forth to the whole community of the elect as the model of virtues. Piously meditating on her and contemplating her in the light of the Word made man, the Church with reverence enters more intimately into the great mystery of the Incarnation and becomes more and more like her Spouse.

—*Lumen Gentium*

It seems a simple formula: To increase in holiness I need only conquer sin. Mother Mary, pray for me to overcome every sin that keeps me from your Son.

April 30

Tell all the people that God gives them graces through her. If only I could put in the heart of everybody that light I have here in my breast to burn and make me love the Heart of Jesus and the Heart of Mary so much!

—Bl. Jacinta Marto

May a brilliant, burning love for God grow stronger in my heart every day.

May 1

The Rosary is my favorite prayer. A marvelous prayer! Marvelous in its simplicity and its depth.

—Pope John Paul II

Today I'll pray the rosary and ask John Paul II to pray for me.

May 2

All things rising, all things sizing
Mary sees, sympathizing
With that world of good,
Nature's motherhood.

—Fr. Gerard Manley Hopkins

Mary, like springtime, you brought new life. By your fiat you gave us the Life that would change all life.

May 3

We need Mary for the conversion of sinners, for the bringing of tepid souls to sanctity, for bringing the millions of non-Christians to Christ.

—St. Maximilian Kolbe

For my ongoing conversion, for the times my soul is tepid, and for the times I've turned away from Christ—Mary, pray for me.

May 4

All the sins of your life seem to be rising up against you. Don't give up hope! On the contrary, call your holy mother Mary, with the faith and abandonment of a child. She will bring peace to your soul.

—St. Josemaría Escrivá

*Hopelessness is not from God. Hold on to hope in all
things today, and trust the Lord.*

May 5

We may well believe that the most sacred Virgin Our Lady received so much pleasure in carrying her little Jesus in her arms, that delight beguiled weariness, or at least made it agreeable; for if a branch of *agnus castus* can solace and unweary travellers, what solace did not the glorious Mother receive in carrying the immaculate Lamb of God?

—St. Francis de Sales

*With Mary as my guide, may I always let "delight beguile the weariness"
that may accompany my vocation.*

May 6

[Mary] is not often thought of. There is a type of religious mind which brushes creatures aside as irrelevant, indeed a distraction from the Absolute. The Absolute did not find them so. The Son died for them; for them the Father spared not his own Son (Rom 8:33).

—F.J. Sheed

*Lord, you bestowed untold dignity on your creatures. Let me approach every human
being with respect and with your love.*

May 7

Would you be so kind as to come here for fifteen days?

—THE BLESSED VIRGIN MARY, TO ST. BERNADETTE
SOUBIROUS AT LOURDES, FRANCE

What is the Blessed Mother asking of me today? May I answer her invitation.

May 8

Our Lady of Angels, Our Lady of Good Counsel, Our Lady of Mercy, Our Lady of Miracles, Our Lady of Perpetual Help, Our Lady of the Star, Our Lady of the Storm, Our Lady, the Queen of All Saints, Our Lady, the Dawn of Christianity.

—TITLES OF THE BLESSED VIRGIN MARY

So many names, so many titles for Our Lady,
but they all come back to this: our mother.

May 9

[Mary's] ascent of Calvary and her standing at the foot of the cross together with the beloved disciple were a special sort of sharing in the redeeming death of her Son.

—POPE JOHN PAUL II

Every pain and loss I endure can also be transformed into a special sort of
sharing when I unite myself to the suffering Christ.

May 10

But how could she suffer? She could suffer like any other mother to see her Son suffer, and more than any other mother because she was better than any other and had a Son more worthy of love.

—F.J. SHEED

The Blessed Mother can understand and pray for any pain I endure,
because she suffered so much herself.

May 11

For a sermon on the Blessed Virgin to please me and do me any good, I must see her real life, not her imagined life. I'm sure that her real life was very simple. [Some sermons] show her to us as unapproachable, but they should present her as imitable, bringing out her virtues, saying that she lived by faith just like ourselves, giving proofs of this from the Gospel, where we read: "And they did not understand the words which He spoke to them" [Luke 2:50].

—St. Thérèse of Lisieux

Lord, help me focus on what was simple and real about Mary's life;
help me fix my eyes today on her virtues so that I can imitate them.

May 12

Don't be afraid of being laughed at.   You will crown all by keeping up the tender love of a little child for the Blessed Virgin and a confiding trust in your Guardian Angel.

—Bl. Théophane Vénard

Christian faith is sometimes ridiculed as being simplistic. It is not simplistic,
but it is simple: Love God, and trust in his providential care.

May 13 | Feast of Our Lady of Fatima

Our Lady did not predict that we would have pleasures, earthly joys, honor, power, or material goods. Nor did she predict that we would become big, important people in this world, which is nothing but illusion, blindness, and vanity, and where every goal is sought with so much anguish, deceit, and injustice. "Do you wish to offer yourselves to God? Will you bear all the sufferings he will send you in order to make reparation for the sins by which he is offended? Will you pray for the conversion of sinners?"

"Yes, we will."

—SISTER LUCIA OF FATIMA

Mary's fiat carried a price, yet she paid it with love and surrender.
Help me, Lord, to do the same.

May 14

The message of Fatima is, in its basic nucleus, a call to conversion and repentance, as in the Gospel.

—POPE JOHN PAUL II

Of what do I need to repent? In what ways do I need to convert?
Lead me, Mary, closer to Jesus.

May 15

O blessed and ever-blessed Virgin, by whose blessing not only is every creature blessed by its Creator, but the Creator is blessed by the creature!

ST. ANSELM OF CANTERBURY

Praise God and the many ways he has blessed my life! May my life
become a blessing to his kingdom.

May 16

Mary's submission to the Father is a triumph of her freedom.

—Fr. Gary Caster

The greatest and most authentic freedom comes from the decision to obey God.

May 17

To be a field for the word means to be earth which allows itself to be absorbed by the seed, which assimilates itself to the seed, renouncing itself so as to make the seed germinate. With her motherhood Mary transfused into it her very substance, body and soul, so that a new life might come forth.... *Mary makes herself completely available as the soil, she allows herself to be used and consumed so as to be transformed into him.*

—Cardinal Joseph Ratzinger (Pope Benedict XVI)

Consume me, Lord, so that all that remains is a soul that labors for you.

May 18

I firmly believe that Mary, according to the words of the Gospel, as a pure Virgin brought forth for us the Son of God and in childbirth and after childbirth remained a pure, intact Virgin. The more the honor and love of Christ increases among men, so much the esteem and honor to Mary should grow.

—Ulrich Zwingli

Mary, ever virgin, in honoring you I honor the Lord who created you and the miracles he ordained.

May 19

Call…[the rosary] spiritual homeopathy if you like. Many a proud spirit has been brought down by it—many a faddy spirit has been made patient by it. Many a queasy spirit has been made strong by it. Many a distracted spirit has become recollected by it. The weak things of this world hath God chosen to confound the strong.

—ARCHBISHOP WILLIAM BERNARD ULLATHORNE

The rosary is simple but powerful. And it simply and powerfully works.

May 20

Mixed with the cry of martyrs, the cry of nature wounded by Grace also ascends—and presumably to heaven. That cry has indeed been legitimized for all believers by the words of the Virgin Mother herself—"Son, why hast thou thus dealt with us? Behold, thy father and I have sought thee sorrowing."

—C.S. LEWIS

You have felt my anguish, Mary, and you know my heart.

May 21

He imbibed, He absorbed into his divine Person, her blood and the substance of her flesh; by becoming man of her, He received her lineaments and features, as the appropriate character in which He was to manifest Himself to mankind. The child is like the parent, and we may well suppose that by His likeness to her was manifested her relationship to Him.

—BL. JOHN HENRY NEWMAN

It's easy to say, "Mary gave birth to Jesus," but the reality of that is hard to fathom.
He took her flesh. Can I grasp that? He gave up that same flesh for me.
What ineffable love!

May 22

A gentle maiden, having lodged a God in her womb, asks as its price: peace for the world, salvation for those who are lost, and life for the dead.

—St. Peter Chrysologus

With Mary I pray today for peace in the world, for the salvation of souls, and for the souls in purgatory.

May 23

In the natural order, one imagines that Christ must have been like His mother—this was one infant, at least, about Whom no question could arise as to which parent He resembled; and she found it, probably, as much of a delight as most mothers find it, that her Son was like her. But that remains in the natural order. In the supernatural order her supreme glory is that she was like her Son.

—F.J. Sheed

Mary, I want to be like your Son.

May 24

May the heart of Mary be in each Christian to proclaim the greatness of the Lord; may her spirit be in everyone to exult in God.

—St. Ambrose

Immaculate Heart of Mary, be with me today as I praise God and his work in my life.

May 25

[B]oth the Church and Mary collaborate to give birth to the Mystical Body of Christ since "both of them are the Mother of Christ, but neither brings forth the whole (body) independently of the other."... Thus love for the Church will become love for Mary, and vice versa, since the one cannot exist without the other.

—POPE PAUL VI, QUOTING BL. ISAAC OF STELLA

My faith cannot be divided into compartments: Jesus, Mary,
and the Church are, by God's choice, intertwined.

May 26

The most humble eyes of Mary, as of a simple and humble dove, with which she forever admired the divine greatness, never lost sight of her own nothingness.

—BL. BARTOLO LONGO

Grant me, Lord, not a false humility that belittles my talents but a true humility
that recognizes you as the source of all graces and gifts.

May 27

When your heart is anxious, turn to Mary and say, "Mary, put my heart at peace." When your mind is too busy, look to Mary and pray, "Mary, settle down my mind." When you want to grow and deepen your life, look to Mary and beg, "Mary, just as you helped Jesus grow in wisdom and grace, help me also to advance on the spiritual path which God has laid out for me."

—FR. ALFRED MCBRIDE

Mary, I know that you, too, sometimes felt anxious and unsettled. Pray for me in every
doubt, and help me to follow your example of trust and submission.

May 28

This is not something optional for Christians. It is not something ornamental in the gospel. Mary is—in a real, abiding, and spiritual sense—our mother. If we are to know the brotherhood of Jesus Christ, we must come to know the mother whom we share with Jesus Christ.

—Scott Hahn

May I never exclude Mary from the family of Jesus—or from my family.

May 29

If the hurricanes of temptation rise against you, or you are running upon the rocks of trouble, look to the star—call on Mary!

—St. Bernard of Clairvaux

Mary, you are a bright star of hope in the midst of my struggles.

May 30

She is his mystical channel, his aqueduct, through which he causes his mercies to flow gently and abundantly.

—St. Louis de Montfort

If I empty myself of "self" daily, I can be a channel of God's grace.
Mary, mystical channel, pray for me.

May 31 | Feast of the Visitation

Blessed are you among women, and blessed is the fruit of your womb!

—St. Elizabeth to Mary, Gospel of Luke 1:42

Mary, you were raised above all women, and yet you served Elizabeth in her need.
Help me to serve with such unselfish love.

June 1

Children have always on their lips their mother's name, and in every fear, in every danger, they immediately cry out, Mother, mother! Ah, most sweet Mary! ah, most loving Mother! this is precisely what thou desirest: that we should become children, and call on thee in every danger.

—St. Alphonsus de Liguori

Holy Mary, Mother of God, your name is always on my lips;
I am ready to call on you in every need.

June 2

One of the reasons I do not write more is that there is always house-work, cleaning, scrubbing, sewing, washing (right now it is cleaning fish), etc., to do. Just as she had to do these things, and probably never neglected them. But then, too, I can see her sitting seemingly idle beside a well on just such a day as this, just thanking Him, with each happy breath.

—Dorothy Day

Holy balance. Thank you, God, for work, for duty, for rest and play,
and for the privilege of praising you through it all.

June 3

How happy I was, Oh good mother, to have the grace to gaze upon you.

—St. Bernadette Soubirous

Sometimes a loving gaze can say more than the most eloquent of orations.

June 4

[H]e is the only Son who was in a position to choose who his mother should be; he could choose therefore what every son would choose if he could, the mother who would suit him best.

—F.J. Sheed

Jesus chose you for all time, Mary. I will choose daily to ask for your holy intercession.

June 5

Were we to present…the image of the purely developed character of spouse and mother as it should be according to her natural vocation, we must gaze upon the Virgin Mary.

—St. Teresa Benedicta of the Cross (Edith Stein)

May I live out my vocation as perfectly as I can, with you, Mary, as my model.

June 6

It was fitting for the Queen of Virgins, by a singular privilege of sanctity, to lead a life entirely free from sin, so that while she ministered to the Destroyer of death and sin, she should obtain the gift of life and justice for all.

—St. Bernard of Clairvaux

Immaculate Mary, do I ponder the fact that you ministered to Christ? What a mission you were entrusted with!

June 7

If I feel the need to complain, I go to a quiet place and complain to the Blessed Virgin Mary. If I can look Mary in the eye (so to speak) and still bring myself to grumble,… then maybe—just maybe—I have something legitimate to complain about.

—Mike Aquilina

Mary, you help me to keep my priorities straight and my blessings counted.

June 8

Virgin of Light, you are the smile of a God who loves us.

—Hymn to Mary

Thank you, Mary, for your radiant light in my life.

June 9

It is her "genius" to have described herself as handmaid and not as mother or bride or helpmate or daughter. In doing so, she embraces each and every form of service that is worthy of God. He can form from her everything that pleases him.

—Adrienne von Speyr

You are a model not only for women, Mary, but for everyone who desires to serve God.

June 10

[Flannery O'Connor] was "greatly taken" with a wooden statue on display in one of the chapels. "It was the Virgin holding the Christ child and both were laughing; not smiling, laughing."

—Paul Elie

Jesus and Mary suffered greatly, but their lives were not devoid of joy. The Crucifixion led to the Resurrection. Help me to remember, Lord, that every crucifixion will lead to a rebirth, and help me embrace the gift of laughter.

June 11

Consider the value of the "hidden" life of Mary. Mary was the wife of St. Joseph and the mother of one child, Jesus. She did not do anything our culture would recognize as significant; she was "just" a homemaker. However, Mary's life was rich; it was full. (Can you imagine her dropping Jesus off at day care so she could do something "important"?)

—Kimberly Hahn

Do I view and treat the raising of children as a holy vocation, worthy of a woman's time?

June 12

O great Mother of God, immense sea of graces and of blessings, I too shall be blessed if I live beneath your protection.

—Bl. Bartolo Longo

May a share of your grace wash over me, Mary. Engulf me with your prayers and love.

June 13

When one seeks out the place of the Virgin Mary in history as it is conceived by humans, her role seems paltry indeed.... But if history finds its final meaning in the saga of sanctity, if the value of human beings can be measured by their closeness to Christ, the Holy One of God, the source of all supernatural life, then suddenly Mary is at the summit.... She is the masterpiece of God, the one who after Christ has been the object of his thought for all eternity.

—Fr. Henri Rondet, s.j.

How could I ever think of you as "just" the mother of Jesus? You are the result of God's artistry—perfectly, immaculately conceived in the mind of God.

June 14

The world was forever changed, and no one knew about it except a humble virgin.

—Alice von Hildebrand

You were not concerned with yourself, Mary, but rather with what you must do. And you did it. Help me, too, to simply do what I must do today.

June 15

Mother Most Amiable, Mother Most Chaste, Mother Most Clement, Mother Most Tender, Mother of a Son So Holy, Mother of All Believers.

—Titles of the Blessed Virgin Mary

Mother in every way—to all—lead us to your holy Son.

June 16

O Jesus, at Holy Communion I become Thy sanctuary, but what a poor dwelling I offer Thee, the King of Heaven and earth! Mayest Thou ever find Mary, Thy Mother, in my heart when I receive Thee!

—FR. LAWRENCE G. LOVASIK

Lord, give me a proper humility, one that recognizes my unworthiness and at the same time rejoices that you make me worthy by your grace.

June 17

Mary of Nazareth sheds light on womanhood as such by the very fact that God, in the sublime event of the Incarnation of his Son, entrusted himself to the ministry, the free and active ministry of a woman.

—POPE JOHN PAUL II

This is equality, created and determined by God:
"Male and female he created them" (Genesis 1:27).

June 18

Mary Immaculate,
Merely a woman, yet
Whose presence, power is
Great as no goddess's
Was deemèd, dreamèd; who
This one work has to do—
Let all God's glory through.

—FR. GERARD MANLEY HOPKINS

You were and you are single-minded, Mary: You aim to bring Christ to the world. I want to do the same.

June 19

Were each woman an image of the Mother of God, a *Spouse of Christ*, an apostle of the divine Heart, then would each fulfill her feminine vocation no matter what conditions she lived in and what worldly activity absorbed her life.

—St. Teresa Benedicta of the Cross (Edith Stein)

Mary listened to the Lord's call and followed. It's that simple and that challenging. Am I listening? Have I followed?

June 20

Her prayers and requests are so powerful with [God] that he accepts them as commands in the sense that he never resists his dear mother's prayer because it is always humble and conformed to his will.

—St. Louis de Montfort

How tender the love between mother and Son! How beautifully conformed to his will is our Mother Mary. Make your will mine today, Lord.

June 21

We used our immortality so badly as to incur the penalty of death: Christ used His mortality so well as to restore us to life. The disease was brought in through a woman's corrupted soul: the remedy came through a woman's virgin body.

—St. Augustine

God always has a cure. We are never beyond his healing hand.

June 22

Are not Jesus and Mary the two sublime loves of the Christian people? Are they not the new Adam and the new Eve whom the tree of the cross unites in sorrow and in love in order to make satisfaction for the guilt of our first parents in Eden?

—Pope Pius XII

The two sublime loves—Jesus and Mary—are inseparable parts of our redemption.

June 23

O Queen of Martyrs, sea of sorrows, do not forsake me when, beneath the burden of suffering, I feel my strength and virtue weakening.

—Bl. Bartolo Longo

When I am weak, Mary, strengthen me with your prayers and with the reminder that you, too, knew sorrow and yet held fast to hope.

June 24

Mary was the most simple of all creatures, and the most closely united to God. Her answer to the angel…contained all the mystic theology of her ancestors to whom everything was reduced, as it is now, to the purest, simplest submission of the soul to the will of God, under whatever form it presents itself.

—Fr. Jean-Pierre de Caussade

It's excruciatingly simple: Say yes to God in all things.

June 25

Honor, revere and respect the Blessed Virgin Mary with a very special love; she is the Mother of our Sovereign Lord, and so we are her children.

—St. Francis de Sales

How can I help but love and honor the mother of Jesus, the woman he loves so much?

June 26

Pure Lady and noble Queen of Heaven and Earth, touch my stony heart with one of thy scalding tears, one of those which thou didst shed in bitter distress for thy tender Child under the wretched cross, so that my heart of stone may be softened, and may hearken to thee.

—Bl. Henry Suso

To what have I hardened my heart? Mary, pray for me to forgive those who have hurt me in any way.

June 27 | Feast of Our Lady of Perpetual Help

There is no sinner, however great, who is lost if Mary protects him.

—St. Bernard of Clairvaux

Mary, you offer hope to the hopeless. Your prayers are our shield.

June 28

And they did not understand the saying which he spoke to them.... And his mother kept all these things in her heart.

—Gospel of Luke 2:50, 51

How often do I speak before I understand? Lord, help me to be still, to ponder and pray.

June 29

When the twelve-year-old Christ is lost in Jerusalem, Mary already begins to experience these pains. She suffers the loss of her son for three days as he is busy conducting his Father's affairs....

All this "pre-enacts" what will take place at the end of Jesus' life.... And Mary will lose her son again, but this time in an even more profound way as he is crucified on Calvary.

—Edward Sri

Mary, your freedom from sin did not prevent you from suffering. Help me to see that suffering is a part of our life in Christ, and that all sufferings, in the end, draw us closer to the Resurrection.

June 30

[T]hose who make a point of announcing to others the glories of Mary are certain of heaven.

—St. Bonaventure

We sing of Mary not for spiritual insurance but out of love for the one who bore Jesus. I want to announce her grace-filled beauty to others every chance I get.

July 1

I remember that, when my mother died, I was about twelve years old—a little less. When I began to understand my loss, I went in my affliction to an image of our Lady, and with many tears implored her to be my mother.... I have by experience found the royal Virgin [to] help me whenever I recommended myself to her.

—St. Teresa of Avila

Mary, your motherhood is not a metaphor: You are a real and powerful mother to me.

July 2

Courage, my sons. Don't you see that we are leaving on a mission? They pay our fare in the bargain. What a piece of good luck! The thing to do now is to pray well in order to win as many souls as possible. Let us, then, tell the Blessed Virgin that we are content, and that she can do with us anything she wishes.

—St. Maximilian Kolbe

St. Maximilian surrendered his life to your care, Mary.
Do I have the courage to do the same?

July 3

I looked at her all I could.

—St. Bernadette Soubirous

I want to continually drink in your presence, Mother—
the presence of peace, hope, trust, and love.

July 4

Our Lady, like all very calm people, had the knack of putting first things first; and before she did anything else, there was a visit to be paid. Among all the words Gabriel had spoken to her, the most significant, surely, and the most awe-inspiring ever addressed to a human being, there was one which had particularly caught her attention; not the one that catches our attention. "Thy cousin Elizabeth also is with child"; that meant action, going to see her and be with her in her confinement; so the day-dreams had to wait. She arose with haste; not with hurry, with haste; calm people don't need to be in a hurry, because they hasten at the right moment, about the right things.

—Monsignor Ronald Knox

Mary, help me always to hasten at the right moments and for all the right things.

July 5

She did and suffered the same things that anyone in a similar state of life might do or suffer. She goes to visit her cousin Elizabeth as her other relatives did. She took shelter in a stable in consequence of her poverty. She returned to Nazareth from whence she had been driven by the persecution of Herod, and lived there with Jesus and Joseph, supporting themselves by the work of their hands. It was in this way that the holy family gained their daily bread. But what a divine nourishment Mary and Joseph received from this daily bread for the strengthening of their faith! It is like a sacrament to sanctify all their moments.

—Fr. Jean-Pierre de Caussade

Mary lived the "sacrament of the moment" every day. Let me strive to do the same.

July 6

Mother of Divine Grace, Mother of Divine Knowledge, Mother of Divine Love, Mother of Divine Pity, Mother of Divine Providence.

—TITLES OF THE BLESSED VIRGIN MARY

Mother, you were offered a unique, spectacular gift of grace and responded to the divine call with faith. Pray that I will also respond to every claim your Son makes on my life.

July 7

I greet you, Lady, Holy Queen, Holy Mary, Mother of God, Virgin who became the Church, chosen by the most holy Father of heaven; consecrated to holiness through His most holy and beloved Son and the Holy Spirit, the Comforter. In you was and is the whole fullness of grace and everything that is good.

—ST. FRANCIS OF ASSISI

You have been raised above all women, Mary, and yet we greet you as friend. Like God's love, your care for us is both transcendent and immanent.

July 8

[S]he devoted herself totally as a handmaid of the Lord to the person and work of her Son.

—*LUMEN GENTIUM*

Help me, Lord, to devote myself totally to the duties and responsibilities you have given me.

July 9

O Mary, mirror of patience, you alone are my help in my temptations.

—BL. BARTOLO LONGO

Come to my aid in every moment of temptation, Mary! Pray with your pure heart that I will remain true to your Son.

July 10

Anyone who has known a mother's love can come to see why our heavenly Father gave us all a common mother in the Blessed Virgin Mary. The truth of Mary's love for me was among the earliest lessons I learned from my mom.

—MIKE AQUILINA

Mary most holy, Mary, my mom. Daily you teach me to love.

July 11

In thy hands are all the treasures of the mercies of God.

—ST. PETER DAMIAN

I place myself in your hands, Mary, and at the Lord's mercy.

July 12

Why should human frailty fear to go to Mary? In her there is no austerity, nothing terrible: she is all sweetness, offering milk and wool to all.

—ST. BERNARD

Gentle Mother, thank you for your sweet and tender care.

July 13

Mary, in bringing forth Jesus, our Savior and our Life, brought forth many unto salvation; and by giving birth to Life itself, she gave life to many.

—ST. WILLIAM THE ABBOT

Our Lady, you are intricately tied to our redemption. With your fiat came the hope of our salvation. Thank you for saying yes.

July 14

She would not have been blessed, though she had borne him in the body, had she not heard the word of God and kept it.

—St. John Chrysostom

As Mary was, I am called to listen to God's word and to respond with love and faith. What is he calling me to today?

July 15

When the storms of temptations rage, the most compassionate Mother of the faithful, with maternal tenderness, protects them as it were in her own bosom until she has brought them into the harbor of salvation.

—Aloysius Novarinus

You shelter us from the storms of the world, Blessed Mother, and walk with us down every rocky path. Lead me to the safety of eternity with your Son.

July 16 | Feast of Our Lady of Mount Carmel

Most beautiful Flower of Mount Carmel, Fruitful Vine, Splendor of Heaven, Blessed Mother of the Son of God, Immaculate Virgin, assist me in this my necessity. O Star of the Sea, help me and show me herein that you are my Mother.

—Chaplet of Our Lady, Star of the Sea

Star of the Sea, your constancy and maternal care assist me every day. Though I'm not worthy of such attention, I am grateful for the gift.

July 17

O Mary, my Mother, be my refuge and my shelter.
Give me peace in the storm. I am tired on the journey.
Let me rest in you. Shelter and protect me.

—ST. BERNADETTE SOUBIROUS

*Mary, you know how hard this earthly life can be; thank you for the rest
and refreshment you provide.*

July 18

Against all human expectation God chooses those who were considered powerless and weak to show forth his faithfulness to his promises: Hannah, the mother of Samuel; Deborah; Ruth; Judith and Esther; and many other women. Mary "stands out among the poor and humble of the Lord, who confidently hope for and receive salvation from him."

—CATECHISM OF THE CATHOLIC CHURCH, #489,
QUOTING *LUMEN GENTIUM*, 55

*Lord, you choose unlikely vessels to manifest your glory. Give me the faith to
follow you, no matter how unlikely your plan for me may seem.*

July 19

[T]he description "blessed among women" would bring to mind the Old Testament heroines Jael and Judith…. Jael and Judith were blessed specifically because the Lord used them to rescue his people from the attacks of their enemies.

Standing in this tradition, Mary is called "blessed among women" because she too will be instrumental in God's plan for saving Israel. However, Mary's role has one crucial difference from those warrior women of old. Mary won't be engaging in a physical battle. Rather, she will participate in God's saving plan through the son she is carrying in her womb.

—EDWARD SRI

Through the simple act of becoming a mother, a woman changed the world.

July 20

The love that this good mother bears us is so great that as soon as she perceives our wants, she comes to our assistance. She comes before she is called.

—RICHARD OF ST. LAWRENCE

Mary, even when I forget to call on you, you are there, anticipating my needs and praying for them.

July 21

When God decided to become man in his Son, he needed the freely spoken "yes" of one of his creatures. God does not act against our freedom. And something truly extraordinary happens: God makes himself dependent on the free decision, the "yes" of one of his creatures; he waits for this "yes."

—POPE BENEDICT XVI

God is waiting for me to say yes to something today. What is it? What will I say?

July 22

It is in Our Lady that God fell in love with Humanity.

—CARYLL HOUSELANDER

Mary is the essence of all that I have the potential to be.

July 23

But standing by the cross of Jesus were his mother, and his mother's sister, Mary, the wife of Clopas, and Mary Magdalene.

—GOSPEL OF JOHN 19:25

Do I stand by Jesus in every moment of my life?

July 24

When Mary sees a sinner at her feet, imploring her mercy, she does not consider the crimes with which he is loaded, but the intention with which he comes: and if this is good, even should he have committed all possible sins, the most loving Mother embraces him, and does not disdain to heal the wounds of his soul; for she is not only *called* the Mother of Mercy, but is so truly and indeed, and shows herself such by the love and tenderness with which she assists us all.

—ST. ALPHONSUS DE LIGUORI

Mary, you see the love I have for your Son, and you see what I share with you: the desire to be with him forever. Please pray for that union, Mother Mary.

July 25

Mary is the Mother of God, but also by God's grace and call she is the spiritual mother of the church and of each Christian.

—ALAN SCHRECK

Blessed. A mother. My Blessed Mother.

July 26

What deep understanding existed between Jesus and his mother? How can we probe the mystery of their intimate spiritual union?

—POPE JOHN PAUL II

I cannot fully fathom the depth of the union between Jesus and Mary. But I can pray for both a deeper understanding and a deeper union with each of them.

July 27

No angel, no saint, can equal her in the multitude and accumulation of heavenly good things.

—ST. BONAVENTURE

Mary, blessed Queen of Heaven and Earth, pray for me to grow closer to heavenly good things.

July 28

O Immaculata, Queen of heaven and earth, refuge of sinners and our most loving mother, God has willed to entrust the entire order of mercy to you. I, N..., a repentant sinner, cast myself at your feet, humbly imploring you to take me with all that I am and have, wholly to yourself as your possession and property. Please make of me, of all my powers of soul and body, of my whole life, death and eternity, whatever most pleases you.

If it pleases you, use all that I am and have without reserve, wholly to accomplish what was said of you: "She will crush your head," and, "You alone have destroyed all the heresies in the world."

—ST. MAXIMILIAN KOLBE, PRAYER OF TOTAL CONSECRATION

Totally yours, Mary. Use me in the battle for souls.

July 29

O Mary,
Mother of Mercy,
watch over all people,
that the Cross of Christ
may not be emptied of its power.

—POPE JOHN PAUL II

May the cross never be a stumbling block for me. Pray, Blessed Mother, that I will always accept the crosses that give meaning to all my suffering.

July 30

Listen, listen, all you who desire the kingdom of God; honor the most Blessed Virgin Mary, and you will find life and eternal salvation.

—ST. BONAVENTURE

Why does honoring Mary lead to life and eternal salvation? Because Mary leads to Jesus, who gives us both.

July 31

Remember, O most gracious Virgin Mary, that never was it known that anyone who fled to your protection, implored your help, or sought your intercession was left unaided.

Inspired by this confidence, I fly unto you, O Virgin of virgins, my mother; to you I come, before you I stand, sinful and sorrowful. O Mother of the Word Incarnate, despise not my petitions, but in your mercy hear and answer me. Amen.

—THE MEMORARE OF ST. BERNARD OF CLAIRVAUX

Good and gracious Mother, hear my prayer and intercede for me, today and always.

August 1

In the light of Mary, the Church sees in the face of women the reflection of a beauty which mirrors the loftiest sentiments of which the human heart is capable: the self-offering totality of love; the strength that is capable of bearing the greatest sorrows; limitless fidelity and tireless devotion to work; the ability to combine penetrating intuition with words of support and encouragement.

—POPE JOHN PAUL II

Our Father deliberately chose as the model of discipleship a woman.
Thus he gave dignity to all women. Thank you, Lord, for all the women
in my life who are sacred gifts to me.

August 2

[W]e call her our mother,… and in the next breath we speak of our holy mother the Church. The truth is that what the Church, the Mystical Body, does in its other members more or less well according to the individual's will to cooperate, she in her single person does continually and perfectly. She is the first steward in the dispensing of graces.

—F.J. SHEED

Mother Mary, Mother Church, you are one. Mary,
Mediatrix of all graces, intercede for me!

August 3

As sailors are guided by a star to the port, so Christians are guided to heaven by Mary.

—St. Thomas Aquinas

Mary, shining light in heaven, beacon in my storms, guide me to Jesus.

August 4

The definition of the Assumption proclaims again the doctrine of our Resurrection, the eternal destiny of each human body, and again it is the history of Mary that maintains the doctrine in its clarity. The Resurrection of Christ can be regarded as the Resurrection of a God, but the Resurrection of Mary foreshadows the Resurrection of each one of us.

—Graham Greene

In life and in death, you show us, Mary, what a true disciple is.

August 5

The light could not be divided from the sun. The light was Mary's soul, rich in grace from the very moment of its creation; and the sun was her immaculate body, in which the Holy Spirit had formed the humanity assumed by the Word.

—Bl. Bartolo Longo

Such a pure and perfect vessel! Lord, make me whole someday in heaven,
as Mary was whole from the moment of her conception.

August 6

O Mary, Mother of sorrows, at the foot of the cross you became our
  mother.

I am a child of your sorrows, a child of Calvary.

Let my heart be united to the cross, to the passion of Jesus Christ,
and teach me not to be afraid of my own trials and crosses.

—St. Bernadette Soubirous

Teach me, Blessed Mother, the same fearlessness that St. Bernadette begged of you.

August 7

Like Mary, our spiritual Mother, we are called to be mediators by
bringing the Word of God to others. Though the Blessed Virgin Mary
is the only person to bring Jesus Christ into the world physically, by
virtue of our baptism each of us is called to bring God's word to others by proclaiming the Good News of salvation.

—Johnnette Benkovic

Am I fulfilling my baptismal call? Who might need to hear
God's Word from me today?

August 8

My children, she is the ladder of sinners, she is my chief confidence,
she is the whole ground of my hope.

—St. Bernard of Clairvaux

Because Mary shows me what I can be, what I should be, what I will be, I hope in her.

August 9

What security did the Blessed Virgin herself have as she fled in the night with the Baby in her arms to go into a strange country? She probably wondered whether St. Joseph would be able to obtain work in a foreign land, how they would get along, and anticipated the loneliness of being without friends, her cousin, St. Elizabeth, her kinfolk.

—Dorothy Day

You lived a "normal" and difficult life in so many ways, Mary. When I wonder, worry, or feel lonely, I will call on you, knowing that you understand.

August 10

Oh, how easy is it for those who love Mary to find her, and to find her full of compassion and love.

—St. Albert the Great

She is waiting for us. We have only to ask for her prayers.

August 11

Penance, penance, penance, pray for the conversion of sinners.

—The Blessed Virgin Mary, to St. Bernadette Soubirous at Lourdes, France

Mary, pray that I will joyfully do penance for the salvation of souls.
What can I give up today?

August 12

For all the salvific influence of the Blessed Virgin on men originates, not from some inner necessity, but from the divine pleasure. It flows forth from the superabundance of the merits of Christ, rests on His mediation, depends entirely on it and draws all its power from it. In no way does it impede, but rather does it foster the immediate union of the faithful with Christ.

—*Lumen Gentium*

No "inner necessity" dictated that Jesus be born of a woman, and yet that is what the Father chose for his Son, for Mary, and for us.

August 13

Eve sought the fruit, but did not find there what she wished for. In her fruit the blessed Virgin found all that Eve had wanted.

—St. Thomas Aquinas

Mary, you are the new Eve who brought us Jesus, our hope and salvation. Lead me to Jesus and to all that I wish for.

August 14

Belief in the Assumption is a source of hope for all Christians because it foreshadows what will one day happen to each faithful Christian. The raising of Mary, body and soul, to the glory of heaven anticipates what will happen at the final judgment to all who are to be saved.

—Alan Schreck

Mary, model of our salvation, I long to be where you are.

August 15 | Feast of the Assumption

We in our exile have sent on ahead of us our advocate who, as mother of our Judge and mother of mercy, will humbly and effectively look after everything that concerns our salvation. Today earth has sent a priceless gift up to heaven, so that by giving and receiving within the blessed bond of friendship, the human is wedded to the divine, earth to heaven, the depths to the heights.... Blessed indeed is Mary, blessed in many ways, both in receiving the Savior and in being received by the Savior.

—St. Bernard of Clairvaux

Mary, my advocate, you stand for everything I am called to be.
Please pray that I will live a life worthy of my Savior.

August 16

And who, I ask, could believe that the ark of holiness, the dwelling place of the Word of God, the temple of the Holy Spirit, could be reduced to ruin? My soul is filled with horror at the thought that this virginal flesh that had begotten God, had brought Him into the world, had nourished and carried Him, could have been turned into ashes or given over to be the food of worms.

—St. Robert Bellarmine

The words of the saints remind me that the Church's teachings are not only
infallible but also perfectly reasonable. Ark of Holiness, pray for me
to be an evangelist for your Son's Church.

August 17

If Mary is believed to be assumed into heaven, it is because we too are one day, by the grace of God, to dwell where she is.

—Fr. Thomas Merton

Mary, I cannot wait to be where you are—in the constant presence of our Lord,
adoring him for all eternity.

August 18

To enter into the mystery of the Blessed Virgin Mary is to take our first steps in the spiritual discipline of trust.

—GEORGE WEIGEL

Pray for me, Mary, when nothing makes sense and it's hard to trust in God's plans.

August 19

Mary lived on the Word of God, she was imbued with the Word of God. And the fact that she was immersed in the Word of God and was totally familiar with the Word also endowed her later with the inner enlightenment of wisdom.

—POPE BENEDICT XVI

*Have I been living on the Word of God? Today
I'll read some Scripture and pray for wisdom.*

August 20

[T]he Father responded to the disobedience of our first parents in the most loving way possible. Even though these human creatures had broken their covenant with him—the sacred family bond of trust—the Father promised a Savior (and a Woman) who would crush the head of Satan.

—SCOTT HAHN

*Mary was in the divine mind from the beginning, destined to be a part of
God's saving plan. What a loving Father we have!*

August 21

Mother of the Author of Grace, Mother of the Church, Mother of the Conqueror, Mother of the Cross, Mother of the Crucified, Mother of the Divine King Jesus Christ.

—TITLES OF THE BLESSED VIRGIN MARY

*Who am I, Lord, that you would share your mother with me?
And yet you do. Thank you for the gift of such a mother.*

August 22 | Feast of the Queenship of Mary

No one has access to the Almighty as His mother has; none has merit such as hers. Her Son will deny her nothing that she asks; and herein lies her power. While she defends the Church, neither height nor depth, neither men nor evil spirits, neither great monarchs, nor craft of man, nor popular violence, can avail to harm us; for human life is short, but Mary reigns above, a Queen forever.

—Bl. John Henry Newman

Mary reigns as Queen; I have nothing to fear.

August 23

And a great sign appeared in heaven, a woman clothed with the sun, with the moon under her feet, and on her head a crown of twelve stars.

—Revelation 12:1

God's Word, God's truth, my hope.

August 24

The life of faith is nothing less than the continued pursuit of God through all that disguises, disfigures, destroys and, so to say, annihilates Him. It is in very truth a reproduction of the life of Mary who, from the Stable to the Cross, remained unalterably united to that God whom all the world misunderstood, abandoned, and persecuted. In like manner faithful souls endure a constant succession of trials.

—Fr. Jean-Pierre de Caussade

Strengthen me in my pursuit of you, God, in spite of every obstacle the world throws in my path. I will cling to the stable and the cross and take heart.

August 25

The Blessed Virgin, by becoming the mother of God, received a kind of infinite dignity because God is infinite; this dignity therefore is such a reality that a better one is not possible, just as nothing can be better than God.

—St. Thomas Aquinas

The dignity of women is affirmed by the role given to and the dignity bestowed upon the Mother of our Lord.

August 26

With all my heart I consecrated myself to the Blessed Virgin Mary, and asked her to watch over me. She seemed to look lovingly on her Little Flower and to smile at her again, and I thought of the visible smile which had once cured me, and of all I owed her.

—St. Thérèse of Lisieux

Like St. Thérèse, I ask you, Mother, to watch over and smile on me always. I owe you so much. Thank you for your constant care.

August 27

Who can repeat her very name without finding in it a music which goes to the heart, and brings before him thoughts of God and Jesus Christ, and heaven above, and fills him with the desire of those graces by which heaven is gained?

—Bl. John Henry Newman

The song that is Mary always points to the divine Composer.

August 28

There is no sinner in the world, however much at enmity with God, who cannot recover God's grace by recourse to Mary, and by asking her assistance.

—St. Bridget of Sweden

Where there is Mary, there is intercession—and hope.

August 29

Mary is not "lost" in the divine Word to which she submits her life, nor is her voice silenced by the action and communication of God. Through the exercise of her freedom, all that is uniquely and personally "Mary" is assumed into the eternal discourse of love that is Father, Son and Holy Spirit.

—Fr. Gary Caster

Submission to God doesn't diminish me but sharpens and defines all that is uniquely "me," just as Mary became who she was meant to be at the moment she said yes to God.

August 30

A good vocation is simply a firm and constant will in which the person who is called must serve God in the way and in the places to which almighty God has called him.

—St. Francis de Sales

Mary, your firm and constant will led you to serve God with your whole heart. May I answer God's call with the same conviction and faith.

August 31

Rejoice then, rejoice, my soul, and be glad in her; for many good things are prepared for those who praise her.

—St. Bonaventure

I imagine a day in heaven when I will be able to see you face-to-face, Mother, I rejoice!

September 1

For as Eve said yes not merely to her own death, but to the death of us all, so Mary said yes, not merely to the birth of a man, but to the rebirth of the whole human race in him whom she knew to be "Son of the Most High" (Lk 1:32).

—MARK SHEA

Every yes and every no reverberate through my life and others' lives.
Give me the grace, Lord, to make holy choices.

September 2

From eternity God foresaw a creature who would in no way, even in the least matter, ever swerve away from him; who would never waste any grace, or appropriate for herself any of the gifts she would receive from him.

—ST. MAXIMILIAN KOLBE

What a powerful thought—to never waste a grace!

September 3

O my Mother, offer me to Jesus.
O my Mother, take my heart and hide it in the heart of Jesus.

—ST. BERNADETTE SOUBIROUS

Immaculate Heart of Mary, be my link to the Sacred Heart of Jesus.

September 4

As flies are driven away by a great fire, so were the evil spirits driven away by her ardent love for God.

—St. Bernardine of Siena

Let my faith burn as brightly as Mary's did, repelling all evil and sin.

September 5

[T]he People of God have learned to call on her as the Consoler of the afflicted, the Health of the sick, and the Refuge of sinners, that they may find comfort in tribulation, relief in sickness and liberating strength in guilt. For she, who is free from sin, leads her children to combat sin with energy and resoluteness.

—Pope Paul VI

In the fight against all sin, Mary, let your strength become mine.

September 6

Mary most holy, Mother of God, passes unnoticed, just as one more among the women of her town.

Learn from her how to live with "naturalness."

—St. Josemaría Escrivá

Mary most holy, and Mary most humble, I want to be as naturally myself as you are.

September 7

[S]he whom God chose to be his mother never existed for an instant without sanctifying grace in her soul.

—F.J. Sheed

I, too, have sanctifying grace in my soul, thanks to baptism. Mary, you are the model of what I can reach for in the battle against my fallen nature.

September 8 | Feast of the Birth of Mary

Today, the reformation of our nature begins, and the aging world is transformed anew to the divine likeness and receives the beginnings of a second formation by God.

—St. Andrew of Crete

Father, you gave us new hope in the New Eve. Thank you for her life
and example and for the gift of new life in Christ.

September 9

It is a sweet and pious belief that the infusion of Mary's soul was effected without original sin; so that in the very infusion of her soul she was also purified from original sin and adorned with God's gifts, receiving a pure soul infused by God; thus from the first moment she began to live she was free from all sin.

—Martin Luther

Help me, Lord, to strive for a life free from sin—to desire the precious
gift that Mary had from the start.

September 10

The title of Mary as our mother is not merely symbolic. Mary *is* our mother in the most real and lofty sense, a sense which surpasses that of earthly maternity. She begot our life of grace for us because she offered up her entire being, body and soul, as the Mother of God.

— St. Teresa Benedicta of the Cross (Edith Stein)

Am I offering my entire being to God? What am I holding back?

September 11

Only after the Last Judgment will Mary get any rest; from now until then, she is much too busy with her children.

—St. John Vianney

Tireless intercessor, thank you for continuing to be a selfless
mother to me, even when I'm a stubborn child.

September 12

In fact, the more I looked at it, the more it seemed to me that God virtually always comes to us through some creature. And when he does that, some glow of his glory is left on the creature, like the radiance on Moses' face (cf. Ex. 34:29–35). But at the same time it remains clear the glory is God's, not something the creature could claim for himself.

—Mark Shea

Mary, you shine with the glory of God, never claiming merit for your virtues.
Help me to always deflect praise and glory to Our Father.

September 13

Mary shares our human condition, but in complete openness to the grace of God. Not having known sin, she is able to have compassion on every kind of weakness. She understands sinful man and loves him with a Mother's love. Precisely for this reason she is on the side of truth and shares the Church's burden in recalling always and to everyone the demands of morality.

—Pope John Paul II

Help me in my weakness, Lord, to live up to your demands.
Buoyed by a mother's love, I can reach for heaven.

September 14

All our perfection consists in being conformed, united, and consecrated to Jesus Christ; and therefore the most perfect of all devotions is, without any doubt, that which most perfectly conforms, unites, and consecrates us to Jesus Christ. Now, Mary being the most conformed of all creatures to Jesus Christ, it follows that of all devotions, that which most consecrates and conforms the soul to our Lord is devotion to His holy Mother, and that the more a soul is consecrated to Mary, the more it is consecrated to Jesus.

—St. Louis de Montfort

Mary, your bond to Jesus is unbreakable, and so my bond to
you is also a link to your Son.

September 15 | Feast of Our Lady of Sorrows

The heart of Mary became, as it were, a mirror of the Passion of the Son, in which might be seen, faithfully reflected, the spitting, the blows and wounds, and all that Jesus suffered.

—St. Lawrence Justinian

An immaculate but wounded heart —Mary, you bore so much for us.

September 16

Queen Conceived Without Original Sin, Queen Crowned With Twelve Stars, Queen of All Peoples, Queen of All Priests, Queen of All Saints, Queen of Heaven's Court, Queen of Humility, Queen of Virtues.

—Titles of the Blessed Virgin Mary

Mary, Queen of Heaven and Earth, who am I that you should hear my prayers?
And yet you hear and intercede. Thank you.

September 17

[O]nce His life-giving finger touched a woman without passing through the ages of interlocked events. Once the great glove of Nature was taken off His hand. His naked hand touched her. There was of course a unique reason for it. That time He was creating not simply a man but the Man who was to be Himself: was creating Man anew: was beginning at this divine and human point, the New Creation of all things.

—C.S. Lewis

Mary's life is a manifestation of God's yearning for our intimate cooperation in his saving work. Lord, I am unworthy of such a love, and yet you offer it to me every day. Glory to you, Lord!

September 18

As Mary bore the Son of God in her womb, she carries with her his message of love, which knows no obstacles and overcomes all short-comings. Our lives…may be disordered, but God nonetheless comes calling. Reaching into the shadows of the caves of our making, God seeks us through his mother.

—Kerry Crawford

My sins are no obstacle to your love, Lord. Are they an obstacle to me? Am I due for confession?

September 19

[T]he fact that the Blessed Virgin Mary, Mother of God and Mother of the Church, received neither the mission proper to the Apostles nor the ministerial priesthood clearly shows that the non-admission of women to priestly ordination cannot mean that women are of lesser dignity, nor can it be construed as discrimination against them. Rather, it is to be seen as the faithful observance of a plan to be ascribed to the wisdom of the Lord of the universe.

—POPE JOHN PAUL II

Lord, in your wisdom you created us to fulfill different roles and purposes.
Every role is vital to the living body of Christ.

September 20

Assuredly, she who played the part of the Creator's servant and mother is in all strictness and truth in reality God's mother and lady and queen over all created things.

—ST. JOHN OF DAMASCUS

Servant, mother, lady, queen—pray for me, Mary, that
I may be all that God has called me to be.

September 21

O Blessed Virgin Mother of God, you shall be my example, I will follow you with all reverence and respect.

—ST. FRANCIS DE SALES

Mary, you are a model for men and women alike—a perfectly devoted disciple.

September 22

Mary is the one creature who unconditionally accepted her creature-liness with all its limitations and weaknesses, with the trust that the Lord, who has seen the humility of His servant, would accomplish great things in her soul.

—ALICE VON HILDEBRAND

Grant me, Lord, a true humility that recognizes you as the source of all greatness.

September 23

Her faith also serves as a model for how we as Christians should follow Christ in our own lives today. Like Mary, we should respond to God's word promptly, joyfully and with a servant's heart—not simply with a passive acceptance, but with an active embrace and hunger to do God's will.

—EDWARD SRI

Am I prompt and joyful? Do I have a servant's heart? Where can I more actively embrace God's will?

September 24

The Mother of God was both a maid and espoused. Virginity and wedlock are honored in her person. She is a challenge to heretics who disparage either one or the other.

—ST. THOMAS AQUINAS

There is no competition among vocations: We are all called to holiness.

September 25

Moreover, saying my prayers there, I noticed behind the high altar a statue of Our Lady, so extraordinary and so different from all I had ever seen before, so much the spirit of my valley, that I was quite taken out of myself and vowed a vow there to go to Rome on Pilgrimage and see all Europe which the Christian Faith has saved.

—HILAIRE BELLOC

Our Lady! How often you are a catalyst, moving us closer to God. You lead us always and everywhere to Jesus Christ.

September 26

Wherein does the Cross that typifies the Lord differ from a cross that does not do so? It is also just the same in the case of the Mother of the Lord. For the honor which we give to her is referred to Him Who was made incarnate of her.

—St. John of Damascus

Honoring Mary is honoring God's plan of redemption.

September 27

Since God has made Mary the new Eve and truly *the Mother of the living,* there are no real orphans, there is no ground for despair; rather is there ground for hope that an appeal may be made from the very sentence pronounced by God. Can a mother ever forget her child, can she ever cease to love him?

—Fr. Omer Englebert

God has not left us alone; we are no longer strangers and sojourners.
We have him, and we have his mother. We are in the best of hands.

September 28

Wire can be bundled up—small and big, new and old, cheap and expensive—but unless the current passes through, there is no light. That wire is just like you and me. Our Lady was the most wonderful wire! She surrendered completely to God, became full of grace, and the current, the grace of God, flowed through her. The moment she was filled with this current, she went to Elizabeth's house to connect that other wire—John—to the current, Jesus. And Elizabeth said, "This child leapt with joy in my womb at your voice."

Let us ask Mary to help make that current within us so that Jesus can use us around the world to connect the hearts of men with the current, Jesus.

—Bl. Teresa of Calcutta

How can I be a living connection, a conduit of the current of Jesus?

September 29

There is no reason why creatures should not be called mediators after a fashion, in that they cooperate in our reconciliation, disposing and ministering to men's union with God.

—St. Thomas Aquinas

*Mary is a mediator in that she prays for my eternal good and hopes for
my union with God. Would my mother ever do less for me?*

September 30

True devotion to Mary takes its rise not from below but from above: not from feelings of affection but from faith. In the first place it means clinging to God and accepting his design.… God has willed to associate Mary with his work of salvation.… It is not for us to set limits to the divine action or to dispense with the intermediaries God has freely chosen.… In God there is room for every kind of superabundance.

—Cardinal Leo Joseph Suenens

*Is there a place in my life where I am trying to limit God's action?
How can I erase those limits?*

October 1

All these with one accord devoted themselves to prayer, together with the women and Mary the mother of Jesus, and with his brethren.

—ACTS 1:14

You were uniquely blessed, Mary, and yet you were a part of the community to which Jesus called you. Help me to prayerfully serve my community.

October 2

Speaking of that Blessed Mother, I must tell you of one of my simple ways. Sometimes I find myself saying to her: "Dearest Mother, it seems to me that I am happier than you. I have you for my Mother, and you have no Blessed Virgin to love.... It is true, you are the Mother of Jesus, but you have given Him to me; and He, from the Cross, has given you to be our Mother—thus we are richer than you! Long ago, in your humility, you wished to become the little handmaid of the Mother of God; and I—poor little creature—am not your handmaid but your child! You are the Mother of Jesus, and you are also mine!"

—ST. THÉRÈSE OF LISIEUX

Mary, you are an undeserved treasure!

October 3

The weapon of the second Eve and Mother of God is prayer.

—BL. JOHN HENRY NEWMAN

Following in your footsteps, Mary, I will arm myself with prayer today.

October 4

Her charity corresponded perfectly to her humility. She who was lowest in her own eyes saw without tremor that she was highest in God's eyes. She was glad of this because He was glad of it, and for no other reason.

—Fr. Thomas Merton

Mary reminds me that my gifts are not my own but are to be used for God's glory.
Every gift is a signpost pointing to Jesus.

October 5

What does motherhood carry with it? Essentially, love and total willingness to serve. Those two things Catholics have always seen in her, telling her their needs with complete confidence, inwardly conversing with her freely.

—F.J. Sheed

I take refuge in your constant and comforting presence, Mother Mary.
Pray that I will imitate your willingness to serve without counting the cost.

October 6

That is, we pray to her; which means that we ask her to pray for us—for all kinds of things, but especially for grace, which is what mattered most to her (matters most to us, too, though we do not always realize it).

—F.J. Sheed

When I don't know what to pray for, when I don't realize what is best, I can simply ask
Mary to pray for me; her intercession brings what is unclear into focus.

October 7 | Feast of Our Lady of the Rosary

The rosary taught Bernadette everything.... The rosary was her dictionary, her spelling book, naming and explaining the mysteries of God's kingdom; it was a map guiding her to the heart of God's love for humanity.

—FR. JOHN LOCHRAN

Through the rosary, Mary, you teach us to love, which is to teach us everything we need to know.

October 8 | Feast of Our Lady of Good Remedy

To ponder the mysteries of the rosary, to enroll in the school of Mary, to find there a new understanding of who Jesus is and what he means to us—this is to share the prayer of the poor and the humble, the prayer of the heart, a peasant's prayer.

—FR. JOHN LOCHRAN

Thank you, Mary, for the gift of the rosary—a prayer for everyone and a remedy for spiritual ills.

October 9

There you are, Caridad del Cobre! It is you that I have come to see; you will ask Christ to make me His priest, and I will give you my heart, Lady: and if you will obtain for me this priesthood, I will remember you at my first Mass in such a way that the Mass will be for you and offered through your hands in gratitude to the Holy Trinity, Who used your love to win me this great grace.

—FR. THOMAS MERTON

You are so inextricably tied to Christ, Blessed Mother, that we cannot help but beg and desire your prayers and to thank you profusely for hastening them to your Son's throne.

October 10

Hail, His palace.

Hail, His tabernacle.

Hail, His robe.

Hail, His handmaid.

Hail, His Mother.

And hail, all holy virtues,

Who, by the grace and inspiration of the Holy Spirit,

Are poured into the hearts of the faithful

So that, faithless no longer,

They may be made faithful servants of God

Through you.

—St. Francis of Assisi

Mary, your life and your calling are almost beyond my comprehension. How blessed and holy you are! Faithless no longer, I want to find him through you.

October 11

O Blessed Rosary of Mary, sweet chain which unites us to God, bond of love which unites us to the angels, tower of salvation against the assaults of Hell, safe port in our universal shipwreck, we will never abandon you.

—Bl. Bartolo Longo

Pray the rosary today! Holy Mary, Mother of God, pray for us sinners now and at the hour of our death.

October 12

The Giver of grace, the Holy Spirit, has dwelt in her soul from the first moment of her existence. He took complete and absolute possession of her, and entered into her to such a degree that the title of Spouse of the Holy Spirit gives us only a remote, feeble, imperfect although true inkling of their relationship.

—ST. MAXIMILIAN KOLBE

I cannot fully grasp the breathtaking work of the Holy Spirit—in Mary's life or mine. But I know that he is real; he is at work in me.

October 13

By her words and her silence the Virgin Mary stands before us as a model for our pilgrim way.

—POPE JOHN PAUL II

Blessed Virgin, pray today that I will know when to speak and when to hold my tongue.

October 14

Some people do not like to take the medicine that would heal them, and call it nonsense. The rosary is exactly that medicine which cures an amazing deal of nonsense.

—ARCHBISHOP WILLIAM BERNARD ULLATHORNE

The rosary—so simple, so ancient, so rich, and so healing.

October 15

To serve Mary and to be her courtier is the greatest honor one can possibly possess, for to serve the Queen of Heaven is already to reign there, and to live under her commands is more than to govern.

—ST. JOHN OF DAMASCUS

Our greatest power is in service. In serving God I find that earthly power means nothing.

October 16

To recite the rosary is nothing other than to *contemplate with Mary the face of Christ.*

—POPE JOHN PAUL II

Help me find time today, Lord, to sit in silence and contemplate your face.
Mary, pray with me and for me.

October 17

The contemplation of Christ has an *incomparable model* in Mary. In a unique way the face of the Son belongs to Mary. It was in her womb that Christ was formed, receiving from her a human resemblance which points to an even greater spiritual closeness. No one has ever devoted himself to the contemplation of the face of Christ as faithfully as Mary.

—POPE JOHN PAUL II

With Mary by my side, let me contemplate the face of Christ—in the Holy Sacrifice of the Mass, in Adoration, in every person I meet.

October 18

On being one day asked by a father of the Society who was going with him to visit a picture of the Blessed Virgin, how much he (St. Stanislaus Kostka) loved Mary—"Father," he replied, "what more can I say? She is my mother." "But," adds the father, "the holy youth uttered these words with such tenderness in his voice, with such an expression of countenance, and at the same time it came so fully from his heart, that it no longer seemed to be a young man, but rather an angel speaking of the love of Mary."

—ST. ALPHONSUS DE LIGUORI

Does my love for Mary show on my face? Does it pour out of my heart? Do I speak tenderly of the mother who loves me so much?

October 19

The Mother of the Church is equally the mother of humanity.... She is forever about the Father's business of assisting those who are longing to know him.

—Fr. Gary Caster

Thank you, Mary, for your tireless effort on my behalf and for helping me to better know your Son.

October 20

From the moment of the Annunciation, the mind of the Virgin-Mother has been initiated into the radical "newness" of God's self-revelation and has been made aware of the mystery. She is the first of those "little ones" of whom Jesus will say one day: "Father,...you have hidden these things from the wise and understanding and revealed them to babes" (Mt. 11:25).

—Pope John Paul II

Make me a little one, Lord.

October 21

Do you want to grow in your relationship with Our Lord? Do you want to be able to say with St. Peter, "Lord, You know everything. You know that I love You"? Then get to know His family. Get to know His Mother.

—Archbishop Timothy M. Dolan

What can I do today, Jesus, to get to know your mother better?

October 22

The Rosary is a teacher of life, a teacher full of gentleness and love, where people beneath the gaze of Mary, almost without noticing, discover they are being slowly educated in preparation for the second life, that which is authentic life, for it is not destined to end in a very few years, but to go on unto eternity.

—BL. BARTOLO LONGO

Lord, you unveil yourself slowly, gently, and powerfully. And all the while your mother quietly intercedes for me. I am overwhelmed by your tender care.

October 23

What Lucifer lost by pride Mary won by humility. What Eve ruined and lost by disobedience Mary saved by obedience.

—ST. LOUIS DE MONTFORT

Obedience leaves me awash in a waterfall of grace.

October 24

I will do everything for heaven for it is my homeland;
there I will find my Mother in all her glory, and with her will enjoy the goodness of Jesus himself.

—ST. BERNADETTE SOUBIROUS

Today, with Mary, I will keep my eyes fixed on Jesus and on my true home.

October 25

Ark of God, Ark of Gold, Ark of Holiness, Ark of the Covenant, Ark That Bears Divinity, Ark That Housed the God of the Covenant, Living and Incorruptible Ark, Living Tabernacle of the Divinity, Living Temple of the Most Holy Trinity.

—TITLES OF THE BLESSED VIRGIN MARY

Lady clothed with the sun and crowned with twelve stars, God-bearer, pray for me.

October 26

In our time Jesus also wants hidden saints like the "woman of Nazareth," who distinguish themselves in nothing exteriorly, but who burn interiorly.

— Fr. Jean du Coeur de Jésus d'Elbée

Mary, pray that I can be like you—quietly ablaze with love for God.

October 27

Sweet blessed beads! I would not part
  With one of you for the richest gem
  That gleams in kingly diadem;
Ye know the history of my heart.

—Fr. Abram Ryan

All that I have prayed for, wanted, offered, suffered, loved, desired, and sacrificed—
in this string of beads is the hope of my soul.

October 28

Though she was the mother of the Lord, yet she desired to learn the precepts of the Lord, and she who brought forth God, yet desired to know God.

—St. Ambrose

I am never so close to God that I can't desire to draw closer.
Make me a lifelong student of your ways, Lord, just as your mother was.

October 29

Just as Mary surpassed in grace all others on earth, so also in heaven is her glory unique. If eye has not seen or ear heard or the human heart conceived what God has prepared for those who love Him [1 Cor. 2:9], who can express what He has prepared for the woman who gave Him birth and who loved Him, as everyone knows, more than anyone else?

—St. Bernard of Clairvaux

Lord, I eagerly await all that you have prepared for me in heaven.
Mary, pray that I stay the course.

October 30

[J]ust as Mary is the Mother of the life of Jesus, so too is she the Mother of our spiritual life. We are not self-starters in the life of faith.

—Monsignor Peter John Cameron, o.p.

I may feel lonely at times, but I am never alone in my faith: Our
Blessed Mother is by my side with prayer and encouragement.

October 31

O most blessed and most sweet Virgin Mary, full of mercy,... obtain [for] me true and perfect love, with which to love thy most beloved Son and my Lord Jesus Christ with my whole heart, and after Him to love thee above all things.

—St. Thomas Aquinas

Mary, you know the shape of "true and perfect love." Mold me with your prayers.

November 1

And when Jesus had finished these parables, he went away from there, and coming to his own country he taught them in their synagogue, so that they were astonished, and said, "Where did this man get this wisdom and these mighty works? Is not this the carpenter's son? Is not his mother called Mary?"

—GOSPEL OF MATTHEW 13:53–55

Mary, how could your extraordinary life appear so ordinary? Teach me humility.

November 2

[S]he now knew the piercing sword of grief, cutting her body and soul. That was her body on the cross, for Jesus, virgin born, had no body other than the body he had received from Mary.

For Mary, from the start, it had ever been thus—this strangeness touched by glory.

—FR. RICHARD JOHN NEUHAUS

There is no resurrection without the cross. May I cling to and trust in the Resurrection as I carry every cross you allow me, Lord.

November 3

Cultivate a special devotion to God's Word, whether studied privately or in public; always listen to it with attention and reverence, strive to profit by it, and do not let it fall to the ground, but receive it within your heart as a precious balm, thereby imitating the Blessed Virgin, who "kept all these sayings in her heart."

—St. Francis de Sales

Mary, may I always ponder God's Word as you did,
knowing that it holds infinite and eternal treasure.

November 4

"I saw her tears flow, how they flowed and flowed, and halfway to the ground, they melted into the light." Thus did Melanie describe Mary's tears at La Salette....

We must recall that, in the final analysis, "Mary's tears melted into pearls of light and that her crucifix was the most brilliant part of the apparition." We need to recall also that...Mary rose from the ground and raised her eyes towards heaven. Only then did her tears cease to flow....

Just as Mary stopped weeping, one day all tears will be dried.

—Fr. Marcel Schlewer

I know that this earth is a valley of tears, but the Lord is waiting for us in the end. His
mother prays for us to persevere and keep our eyes fixed on heaven.

November 5

In giving birth you kept your virginity; in your Dormition you did not leave the world, O Mother of God, but were joined to the source of Life. You conceived the living God and, by your prayers, will deliver our souls from death.

—Byzantine Liturgy

Mary, you are the icon of all that we are called to be.

November 6

My soul, if in death you wish to experience Mary the Mother of love, in life be a faithful child of Mary's love.

—Bl. Bartolo Longo

This life is our training ground for real life. I want to be a faithful
student of your mother, Lord.

November 7

Mary, our Mother, truly desires the best for her children. The best gift we can receive is the power to live immaculately as she did. We can only know the fullness of that gift in heaven, but through Mary's intercession we can begin to realize it while we're still here on earth.

—Fr. Michael Scanlan

Baby steps. I teeter toward heaven, one step at a time.
Steady me, Lord, with the prayers of your mother.

November 8

Everyone's prayers can help others, but the holier, the more.... All are meant to take a part in his redeeming work, but Mary above all; for she was sinless, she was wholly love, she suffered supremely.

—F.J. Sheed

Mary, the best of all possible intercessors, I turn to you today with every need.

November 9

For God has committed to Mary the treasury of all good things, in order that everyone may know that through her are obtained every hope, every grace, and all salvation. For this is His will, that we obtain everything through Mary.

—Pope Pius IX

Mary, mediatrix of all graces, pray for me, that I will receive every
hope, grace, and salvation.

November 10

But oh! Queen of all grace and counsel,
Cause of our joy, Oh Clement Virgin, come:
Show us those eyes as chaste as lightning,
Kinder than June and true as Scripture.
Heal with your looks the poisons of the universe,
And claim your Son's regenerate world!

—FR. THOMAS MERTON

Mary, the purity and beauty of your soul are hard to grasp.
May your prayers heal the ugliness and wounds of this world.

November 11

She has surpassed the riches of the virgins, the confessors, the martyrs,
the apostles, the prophets, the patriarchs, and the angels, for she herself is the first-fruit of the virgins, the mirror of confessors, the rose of
martyrs, the ruler of apostles, the oracle of prophets, the daughter of
patriarchs, the queen of angels.

—ST. BONAVENTURE

You are first in all things, Queen of Heaven, and the example of all that I can be.

November 12

Vessel Blest, Vessel Full of Grace, Vessel of All Perfection, Vessel of
Election, Vessel of Honor. Vessel of Singular Devotion, Precious Vessel
of Untold Graces.

—TITLES OF THE BLESSED VIRGIN MARY

You were the vessel chosen to bear the Son of God. How did you say yes?
Mary, give me your faith.

November 13

This is why the blessed Virgin is called powerful—nay, sometimes, all-powerful, because she has, more than anyone else, more than all angels and saints, this great, prevailing gift of prayer. No one has access to the Almighty as His Mother has.

—BL. JOHN HENRY NEWMAN

He listens to you, Mary. Beg for me all graces, and help me to grow in the gift of prayer.

November 14

When we see her, we see our own human nature at its purest. She is not the sun, dazzling our weak sight by the brightness of its rays. Rather, she is fair and gentle as the moon, which receives its light from the sun and softens it and adapts it to our limited perception.

—ST. LOUIS DE MONTFORT

We cannot see God face-to-face in this world, so he has given us you, Mary. You show us that union between the human and the divine is possible.

November 15

It is important to understand what is meant by the title, "our Blessed Mother." Mary is not spiritual mother of men solely because she was physical Mother of the Savior.... Mary consented in faith to become the Mother of Jesus.... She conceived in her heart, with her whole being, before she conceived in her womb. First came Mary's faith, then her motherhood.

—-NATIONAL CONFERENCE OF CATHOLIC BISHOPS

Give me faith first, Lord, above all things. Everything else will follow.

November 16

The knot of Eve's disobedience was loosed by the obedience of Mary. What the virgin Eve had bound in unbelief, the Virgin Mary loosed through faith.

—St. Irenaeus of Lyons

Our Lady Who Unties Knots, pray for us! Help me to be faithful and obedient today.

November 17

Mary's grace all comes from Jesus. That's what makes her so powerful in God's family. No one ever honored his mother like Jesus; he now wants us to imitate him.

—Scott Hahn

Mary, you are the mother of Jesus, and he loved you with a child's love.
Can I do less than my Lord did?

November 18

Upon these two titles, Mary Mother of God, and Mary the Mother of mankind, the whole practice of the Catholic's devotion to the Blessed Virgin Mary is built.

—Archbishop Alban Goodier

His mother, my mother, now and in heaven. An undeserved and humbling gift.

November 19

Through her we may see him
Made sweeter, not made dim.

—Fr. Gerard Manley Hopkins

Mary, you do not eclipse our Lord but sharpen and define our
vision of his love and goodness.

November 20

By her maternal charity, Mary cares for the brethren of her Son who still journey on earth surrounded by dangers and difficulties, until they are led to their happy fatherland.

—*Lumen Gentium*

Jesus did not leave us alone: He sent His Holy Spirit, the Advocate, and his mother's prayers. Holding tightly to these anchors, I cannot drift away from him.

November 21

It was so tremendous, yet so passive.

She was not asked to do anything herself, but to let something be done to her. She was not asked to renounce anything, but to receive an incredible gift. She was not asked to lead a special kind of life, to retire to the temple and live as a nun, to cultivate suitable virtues or claim special privileges.

She was simply to remain in the world, to go forward with her marriage to Joseph, to live the life of an artisan's wife, just what she had planned to do when she had no idea that anything out of the ordinary would ever happen to her.

—Caryll Houselander

Lord, let my faith be as tremendous and as passive as Mary's! Let me simply go forward in faith, to live my vocation and to do your will.

November 22

Always go to Jesus through Mary, but not for fear of Jesus…but because it is his plan of love. In the same way that he himself came through Mary, he wants us to go to him through Mary. It is the surest way, the most direct way, the sweetest way, too. Why? Because we find Jesus in the arms of Mary.

—Fr. Jean du Coeur de Jésus d'Elbée

Jesus is never really separated from Mary. He wants us, too, to embrace her and find comfort in her arms.

November 23

We do not need to deny the reality of evil either within us or around us. Mary invites us to face it and to transform it.

—Fr. John Lochran

In the face of evil and even my own sin, you help me, Mary,
with Pope John Paul II to say, "Be not afraid!"

November 24

Holy Mary, Mother of God,
you have given the world its true light,
Jesus, your Son—the Son of God.
You abandoned yourself completely
to God's call
and thus became a wellspring
of the goodness which flows forth from him.
Show us Jesus. Lead us to him.
Teach us to know and love him,
so that we too can become
capable of true love
and be fountains of living water
in the midst of a thirsting world.

—Pope Benedict XVI

Following you, Mary, is following perfection in discipleship.
How can I know and love Jesus perfectly, as you did?
How can I be more capable of true love?
Pray for me today, Mary, to see what I must do.

November 25

In the Eastern Churches they say that when Saint Andrew died and went to heaven, his brother Peter was already on the job. Andrew said to Peter, "Where is she?" Peter understood that he was asking for Our Lady. He replied, "Andrew, she's not up here in heaven. She's down on earth, drying the tears from the eyes of her children in the valley of tears."

—FR. ANDREW APOSTOLI, C.F.R.

When I mourn and weep, Mary is here, with comfort and hope for me.

November 26

When the Holy Spirit, her spouse, finds Mary in a soul, he hastens there and enters fully into it. He gives himself generously to that soul according to the place it has given to his spouse.

—ST. LOUIS DE MONTFORT

To honor Mary is to honor God's wishes.

November 27

Is not the Blessed Virgin the best of all mothers?

—ST. JUST DE BRETENIÈRES

Mothers love, guide, protect, care for, pray, teach, nourish, dry tears, listen, frown, encourage, share, warn, laugh, and rejoice. Thank you, Mother.

November 28

The example of *Mary* is relevant here. She is the ideal type of woman who knew how to unite tenderness with power. *She stood under the cross.*

—ST. TERESA BENEDICTA OF THE CROSS (EDITH STEIN)

*Give me the strength to stand under every cross,
Lord, knowing that I am at your feet.*

November 29

Marvel at the courage of Mary—at the foot of the cross, in the greatest human sorrow (there is no sorrow like hers) filled with fortitude.

And ask her for that same fortitude, so that you, too, will know how to remain close to the cross.

—St. Josemaría Escrivá

When I require fortitude, do I rely on myself or on the Lord's strength?
Mary, pray for me.

November 30

Is Mary Calling You?

—North American Lourdes Volunteer sign

I'm listening, Mary. What do you want me to hear today?
What do you want me to do today?

December 1

Her very image is as a book in which we may read at a glance the mystery of the Incarnation, and the mercy of the Redemption; and withal her own gracious perfections also, who was made by her Divine Son the very type of humility, gentleness, fortitude, purity, patience, love.

—BL. JOHN HENRY NEWMAN

To read the book of Mary is to read God's love letter to me.

December 2

"Behold a virgin shall conceive and bear a son,
          and his name shall be called Emmanuel"
(which means, God with us).

—GOSPEL OF MATTHEW 1:23

Our Lady's cooperation with the Holy Spirit brought us the gift of God's immanence.
Thank you, Lady, for saying yes.

December 3

There is little doubt that we are passing through a period marked by a lack of interest in the saints. Much more is involved here than devotion to the saints, even St. Mary. What is at stake is the reality of the humanity of the risen Jesus. There is danger of so spiritualizing the risen Christ that we diminish awareness of His humanity.... Father Karl Rahner declared that the special temptation that affects Christians today, Catholics and Protestants alike, is the temptation to turn the central truths of the faith into abstractions, and abstractions have no need of mothers.

—NATIONAL CONFERENCE OF CATHOLIC BISHOPS

Jesus required a mother; I do too. Let my devotion to you, Mother, be
concrete and real, as your connection to Jesus is.

December 4

The gift of his mother was the final gift that he was giving mankind as the fruit of his sacrifice…a gesture intended to crown his redemptive work.

—Pope John Paul II

Blessed Mother, crown jewel of Christ's work, be my light and inspiration.

December 5

It was by power from Him that Mary was able
to bear in her bosom who bears all things up!
…
She gave Him milk from Himself who prepared it,
she gave Him food from Himself who made it!

—St. Ephrem of Syria

Mary, you knew that all gifts are from God, given to glorify him. What are my gifts? Am I using them to reveal God's glory?

December 6

Who seeks without her aid, attempts to fly without wings.

—St. Antonius

Am I flying without wings today? Mary, help me to soar.

December 7

Because he was God, he could give his mother gifts not only before he was born of her, but before she was born herself. This is the meaning of the doctrine of the Immaculate Conception.

—F.J. Sheed

In creating a pure and perfect mother, Lord, and in saving her before she was born, you gave us hope for what we can become.

December 8 | Feast of the Immaculate Conception

Truly Gabriel was speaking with the "Queen of the Angels." By divine grace Mary, who looked like a perfectly ordinary Palestinian girl, had been kept immaculate, free from the stain of original sin since her conception. She would be the one to give birth to the Lord. She was the culmination of Israel. She was the Israelite who at last answered a perfect yes to all God's plans.

—MIKE AQUILINA

What is my perfect yes?

December 9

O, how little known the Immaculate Virgin still is! When will the souls of men love the Divine Heart of Jesus with her Heart, and in the presence of His Heart love the Heavenly Father?

—ST. MAXIMILIAN KOLBE

May I love my Lord today with all the tender love of a mother's heart.

December 10

While Mary holds your hand, you cannot fall; under her protection you have nothing to fear; if she walks before you, you shall not grow weary; if she shows you favor, you shall reach the goal.

—ST. BERNARD OF CLAIRVAUX

Mary, I give you my hand to hold today. Help me to reach my goal.

December 11

In her, the destinies of the world were to be reversed, and the serpent's head bruised. In her was bestowed the greatest honor ever put upon any individual of our fallen race. God was taking upon Him her flesh, and humbling Himself to be called her offspring—such is the deep mystery!

—BL. JOHN HENRY NEWMAN

In the midst of mystery, Lord, you give me something real and solid
—a mother to cling to.

December 12 | Feast of Our Lady of Guadalupe

You need not be afraid, am I not here?

—THE BLESSED MOTHER, TO ST. JUAN DIEGO

You are indeed here with me now, Mary, praying for me.
For today I will not fear a thing.

December 13

(Mary) obeys the orders of St. Joseph, she takes the divine Child in her arms, and with him goes to meet privations and sacrifices…. She goes out towards an uncertain future, without knowing how long it will last. She first goes with him to Egypt, later to Nazareth, resigned and full of trust, to give us an example of resignation and obedience. Jesus is her strength. In our difficult hours, may she remind us of Jesus, guide us and protect us…. In our bitter hours let us recall the flight of Jesus into Egypt. Let us picture Mary and Joseph who suffer because they were specially beloved of Jesus.

—BL. TITUS BRANDSMA

Help me, Jesus, to remember that I can unite all my suffering to your suffering, thus giving my pain meaning. You renew my hope in my most difficult hours.

December 14

The Virgin, weighed
With the Word of God,
Comes down the road:
If only you'll shelter her.

—ST. JOHN OF THE CROSS

Let me shelter you in my heart, Mary, and always keep you close.

December 15

We implore our Mother's help always, everywhere, and for everything. We pray to her to be enlightened in our doubts, to be put back on the right path when we go astray, to be protected when we are tempted, to be strengthened when we are weakening, to be lifted up when we fall into sin, to be encouraged when we are losing heart, to be rid of our scruples, to be consoled in the trials, crosses and disappointments of life.

—St. Louis de Montfort

Mother Mary, you can help me in every circumstance.
I implore your aid today in all things!

December 16

Mary, as the pattern both of maidenhood and maternity, has exalted woman's state and nature, and made the Christian virgin and the Christian mother understand the sacredness of their duties in the sight of God....

What Christian mother can look upon her image and not be moved to pray for gentleness, watchfulness, and obedience like Mary's? What Christian maiden can look upon her without praying for the gifts of simplicity, modesty, purity, recollection, gentleness such as hers?

—Bl. John Henry Newman

May I always treat my duties as sacred, whatever my station in life.

December 17

Virgin Blessed Above All Things, Virgin Bright, Virgin Chaste and Pure, Virgin Clothed With the Sun, Virgin Ever Meek, Virgin Ever Pure, Virgin Mother of the Messiah Jesus.

—Titles of the Blessed Virgin Mary

Ever Virgin, ever my mother. In you, Mary, a seeming paradox became
a reality and an indispensable part of my faith.

December 18

[N]o other story, no pagan legend or philosophical anecdote or historical event, does in fact affect any of us with that peculiar and even poignant impression produced on us by the word Bethlehem.

—G.K. CHESTERTON

The reality of Bethlehem is Christ with us. Bethlehem is Christ's
gift to Mary and Mary's gift to us.

December 19

You, O great Mother of God, are the enclosed garden, into which the hand of a sinner never entered to gather its flowers. You are the beautiful garden in which God has planted all the flowers that adorn the Church, and amongst others the violet of your humility, the lily of your purity, the rose of your charity.

—ST. BERNARD OF CLAIRVAUX

Mary most humble, pure, and loving, you are a perfect bouquet.

December 20

Our understanding of Our Blessed Lady depends totally upon our understanding of her Son. Everything about her flows from her being Christ's mother; as our understanding of him grows, our understanding of her grows.

—F.J. SHEED

May I grow daily in my understanding of you, Lord, and of your mother,
to whom you are inextricably connected.

December 21

O, Mary, did you not find a room for your Son? Here it is, I offer it to you in this heart of mine. It is cold and unworthy, truly: but are you not the Mother of God? the Almighty through grace? the Dispenser of all gifts? Do change this heart of mine and make it like yours.

—Bl. Bartolo Longo

Let me, Lord, always have room in my heart for you and for the woman you chose to be your mother and mine.

December 22

If the world wanted what is called a non-controversial aspect of Christianity, it would probably select Christmas. Yet it is obviously bound up with what is supposed to be a controversial aspect (I could never at any stage of my opinions imagine why): the respect paid to the Blessed Virgin.... You cannot visit the child without visiting the mother; you cannot in common human life approach the child except through the mother. If we are to think of Christ in this aspect at all, the other idea follows as it is followed in history.... [T]hose holy heads are too near together for the haloes not to mingle and cross.

—G.K. Chesterton

Proper veneration of Mary is simply respect for God's choice and his will.

December 23

Immensity cloistered in thy dear womb,
Now leaves His well-belov'd imprisonment,
There He hath made Himself to His intent
Weak enough, now into the world to come;
But O, for thee, for Him, hath the inn no room?

—John Donne

I cannot imagine, Lord, what Mary felt when she was turned away from the inn.
Do I have room for your mother, or have I turned her away?

December 24

There fared a mother driven forth
　　　Out of an inn to roam;
In the place where she was homeless
　　　All men are at home.
The crazy stable close at hand,
With shaking timber and shifting sand,
Grew a stronger thing to abide and stand
　　　Than the square stones of Rome.

—G.K. CHESTERTON

From seeming weakness came ineffable strength; from simplicity and poverty, the greatest wealth the world has ever known. Thank you, Mary. Thank you, Jesus.

December 25 | Christmas Day

Christ the Lord is born today; today, the Savior has appeared. Earth echoes songs of angel choirs, archangels' joyful praise. Today on earth his friends exult: Glory to God in the highest, alleluia.

—ROMAN BREVIARY, CHRISTMAS, ANTIPHON AT SECOND VESPERS

*Today, Mary, we gaze upon the gift you gave when you said yes.
Thanks be to God! Alleluia!*

December 26

Magnify, my soul, her who is more honorable and glorious than the hosts above. I behold a mystery strange and wondrous. The cave is heaven, the Virgin is the throne of the cherubim, the manger is the place where the Incomprehensible is laid, Christ our God, Whom we magnify with song.

—BYZANTINE MENAEA, FEAST OF THE NATIVITY,
CANON AT MATINS, NINTH ODE

You asked the incomprehensible of Mary, and she said, "Let it be done...." In this Christmas season, Lord, and always, may I echo her fiat.

December 27

To take Mary as my model in all that I do, asking myself what Mary has done, and how and why she did it.

—St. Catherine Labouré

What you did, Mary, was simple in its way: You obeyed. But how? By God's grace.
And why? For love of him. Let me follow your simple way.

December 28

"God hath chosen her and forechosen her," it says in the Office. In God is all eternity, and from eternity was Mary destined to bear under her heart Him…"whom earth and sea and sky honor, worship and preach."

—Sigrid Undset

You chose and you foresee my destiny, Father, but still I have the gift of free will, to
say yes or no. Mary, pray for me to say yes, to bear all that God asks of me.

December 29

What a wonder is Your mother! The Lord entered her, and became a Servant; the Word entered her, and became silent within her; Thunder entered her, and His voice was still; the Shepherd of all entered her, and He became a Lamb in her, and came forth bleating.

—St. Ephrem of Syria

Mary's life and role were supernatural, and yet she was human, as I am.
Lord, enter my life and become my all.

December 30

Mary, my dearest mother,
Give me your heart
So beautiful, so pure, so Immaculate, so full of love
And humility, that I may
Receive Jesus as you did—
And go in haste to give him
To others.

—BL. TERESA OF CALCUTTA

Mary, you received Jesus as a gift and gave him to the world.
Let me use my gifts too, to show Jesus to everyone I meet.

December 31

Mary was, so to speak, "at home" with God's word, she lived on God's word, she was penetrated by God's word. To the extent that she spoke with God's words, she thought with God's words, her thoughts were God's thoughts, her words, God's words. She was penetrated by divine light and this is why she was so resplendent, so good, so radiant with love and goodness.

—POPE BENEDICT XVI

Mother of my Savior, mother of us all, precious giver of precious gift—
Mary, lead me to God's word.

: N O T E S :

January

1. Pope John Paul II, *Prayers and Devotions*, Peter Canisius and Johannes van Ierde, eds. (New York: Penguin, 1998), p. 59.

2. Alan Schreck, *Catholic and Christian: An Explanation of Commonly Misunderstood Catholic Beliefs* (Ann Arbor, Mich.: Servant, 1984), p. 188.

3. Peter Kreeft, *Making Sense Out of Suffering* (Ann Arbor, Mich.: Servant, 1986), p. 145.

4. G.K. Chesterton, *Autobiography*, quoted in John Chapin, ed., *The Book of Catholic Quotations* (New York: Farrar, Strauss and Cudahy, 1956), p. 102.

5. John Hardon, S.J. *Retreat with the Lord, A Popular Guide to the Spiritual Exercises of Ignatius of Loyola* (Ann Arbor, Mich.: Charis, 1993), p. 91.

6. Gospel of Matthew 2:10–11.

7. Josemaría Escrivá, *The Way*, no. 516, in *The Way/Furrow/The Forge* (New York: Scepter, 1988), p. 125.

8. Bernard of Clairvaux, adapted from *Doctor Mellifluus*, no. 31, www.vatican.va.

9. Teresa of Calcutta, *Thirsting for God: A Yearbook of Prayers and Meditations*, Angelo D. Scolozzi, ed. (Ann Arbor, Mich.: Charis, 2000), p.139.

10. Titles of the Blessed Virgin Mary, *The Mary Page*, http://campus.udayton.edu.

11. Peter Kreeft, *Making Choices: Practical Wisdom for Everyday Moral Decisions* (Ann Arbor, Mich.: Servant, 1990), p. 216.

12. Thérèse of Lisieux, *Story of a Soul: The Autobiography of St. Thérèse of Lisieux*, John Clarke, trans. (Washington, D.C.: ICS, 1976), pp. 242–243.

13. Adrienne von Speyr, *Confession*, Douglas W. Stott, trans. (San Francisco: Ignatius, 1986), p. 29.

14. Gemma Galgani, quoted in Jill Haak Adels, *The Wisdom of the Saints: An Anthology* (New York: Oxford University Press, 1987), p. 19.

15. Dorothy Day, "About Mary," in *Selected Writings: By Little and by Little*, Robert Ellsberg, ed. (Maryknoll, N.Y.: Orbis, 1992), p. 159.

16 Avery Dulles, *Mary at the Dawn of a New Millennium* (New York: Fordham University, 1998), p, 17.

17 Ambrose, *Concerning Virginity*, bk. 2, chap. 2, no. 7, in Philip Schaff and Henry Wace, eds., *Ambrose: Selected Works and Letters*, vol. 10, *The Nicene and Post-Nicene Fathers, Series 2*, www.ccel.org.

18 Teresa of Avila, *The Interior Castle,* Benedictines of Stanbrook, trans. (London: Baker, 1921), chap. 7, no. 15, www.ccel.org.

19 Pope John Paul II, *Prayers and Devotions,* p. 134.

20 Bonaventure, quoted in Adels, p. 18.

21. Caryll Houselander, "A Secret Form of Virgin Emptiness," in Wendy M. Wright, ed. *Caryll Houselander: Essential Writings* (Maryknoll, N.Y.: Orbis, 2005), p. 101.

22. John Lochran, *The Miracle of Lourdes: A Message of Healing and Hope* (Cincinnati: St. Anthony Messenger Press, 2008), p. 80.

23. Kimberly Hahn, *Life-Giving Love: Embracing God's Beautiful Design for Marriage* (Ann Arbor, Mich.: Charis, 2001), pp. 120–121.

24. Jerome, quoted in Hardon, pp. 222–223.

25. Louis of Blois, *Spiritual Works of Louis of Blois,* John Edward Bowden, ed. (New York: Benziger, 1903), www.ccel.org.

26. Francis de Sales, *The Mystical Flora of St. Francis de Sales* (Dublin: M.H. Gill and Son, 1891), p. 65.

27. Gary Caster, *Mary, In Her Own Words* (Cincinnati: Servant, 2006), p. 45.

28. Robert Bellarmine, quoted in Hardon, p. 70.

29. Edward Sri, *The New Rosary in Scripture: Biblical Insights for Praying the 20 Mysteries* (Ann Arbor, Mich.: Charis, 2003), pp. 71–72.

30. Genevieve Kineke, *The Authentic Catholic Woman* (Cincinnati: Servant, 2006), p. 146.

31. Mark Shea, *By What Authority? An Evangelical Discovers Catholic Tradition* (Huntington, Ind.: Our Sunday Visitor, 1996), p. 146.

February

1. Donna-Marie Cooper O'Boyle, *Grace Café* (North Haven, Conn. : Circle, 2008), p. 57.

2. Gospel of Luke 2:29–33.

3. Thérèse of Lisieux, *St. Thérèse of Lisieux: Her Last Conversations*, John Clarke, trans. (Washington, D.C.: ICS, 1977), p. 166, quoted in Cynthia Cavnar, ed., *Spiritual Treasures from St. Thérèse of Lisieux: A Book of Reflections and Prayers* (Ijamsville, Md.: Word Among Us, 2007), pp. 158–159.

4. Jacques Bur, "Mary's Divine Motherhood," from *The Marian Era: World Annual of the Queen of the Universe* (Chicago: Franciscan Herald, 1969), vol. 9, p. 29.

5. Robert Bellarmine, quoted in Hardon, p. 58.

6. Anthony Mary Claret, quoted in Adels, p. 18.

7. Immaculée Ilibagiza, *Left to Tell: Discovering God Amidst the Rwandan Holocaust* (Carlsbad, Calif.: Hay House, 2006), p. 211.

8. Francis de Sales, *Mystical Flora*, p. 64.

9. Teresa of Avila, *The Way of Perfection*, E. Allison Peers, trans. (New York: Image, 1964), chap. 13, www.ccel.org.

10. Day, "About Mary," in *Selected Writings*, p. 161.

11. Bernadette Soubirous, quoted in Lochran, pp. 39–40.

12. Titles of the Blessed Virgin Mary, *The Mary Page*.

13. Flannery O'Connor, Letter to Dr. T.R. Spivey, in *Collected Works*, Sally Fitzgerald, ed. (New York: Literary Classics of America, 1988), p. 1077.

14. George Weigel, *Letters to a Young Catholic* (New York: Basic, 2004), p. 62.

15. Bernard of Clairvaux, Sermon I, *Vigil. Nativ. Domini*, 5, quoted in Chapin, *The Book of Catholic Quotations*, p. 88.

16. Gabriel Possenti, quoted in Adels, p. 19.

17. C.S. Lewis, *Miracles: A Preliminary Study* (New York: MacMillan, 1960), p. 116.

18. The Blessed Virgin Mary to Bernadette Soubirous, quoted in Lochran, p. 1.

19. Ambrose, *De Virginibus*, 2, 6, quoted in Chapin, *The Book of Catholic Quotations*, p. 92.

20. Bonaventure, quoted in Alphonsus de Liguori, *The Glories of Mary* (New York: Edward Dunigan and Brother, 1852), p. 101.

21. Teresa of Avila, *The Way of Perfection*, www.ccel.org.

22. Caryll Houselander, quoted in John Chapin, ed., *A Treasury of Catholic Reading* (New York: Farrar, Straus and Cudahy), p. 44.

23. Catherine Labouré, quoted in Omer Englebert, *Catherine Labouré and the Modern Apparitions of Our Lady*, Alastair Guinan, trans. (New York: P.J. Kenedy, 1958), p. 126.

24. Pope John Paul II, *Crossing the Threshold of Hope* (New York: Knopf, 1994), p. 45.

25. Alphonsus de Liguori, *Uniformity with God's Will*, Thomas W. Tobin, trans., www.ccel.org.

26. Caster, p. 44.

27. Bernardine of Siena, quoted in Alphonsus de Liguori, *The Glories of Mary*, p. 11.

28. Escrivá, *The Way*, no. 492, *The Way/Furrow/The Forge*, p. 121.

March

1. Early Christian text, quoted in Schreck, *Catholic and Christian*, p. 182.

2. Concepcion Cabrera de Armida, quoted in Paul Thigpen, *A Dictionary of Quotes from the Saints* (Ann Arbor, Mich.: Charis, 2001), p. 250.

3. Titles of the Blessed Virgin Mary, *The Mary Page*.

4. Thomas Merton, *New Seeds of Contemplation* (New York: New Directions, 1972), p. 171.

5. Maximilian Kolbe, quoted in John Hardon, "Maximilian Kolbe, Apostle of Mary," Great Catholic Books Newsletter, vol. 2, no. 3, www.ewtn.com.

6. Ignatius of Antioch, quoted in Thigpen, p. 142.

7. Murray Bodo, *Mystics: Ten Who Show Us the Ways of God* (Cincinnati: St. Anthony Messenger Press, 2007), pp. 9–10.

8. Julian of Norwich, quoted in Bodo, p. 52.

9. Thérèse of Lisieux, *Story of a Soul,* Clarke, trans., p. 243.

10. Scott Hahn, *Hail, Holy Queen: The Mother of God in the Word of God* (New York: Doubleday, 2001), p. 85.

11. Bridget of Sweden, quoted in Thigpen, p. 145.

12. John H. Hampsch, *The Healing Power of the Eucharist* (Ann Arbor, Mich.: Charis, 1999), p. 152.

13. Lochran, p. 80.

14. Josephine Nobisso, *Take It to the Queen: A Tale of Hope* (Westhamptom Beach, N.Y.: Gingerbread House, 2008).

15. Just de Bretenières, quoted in James A. Walsh, ed., *Thoughts from Modern Martyrs* (Ossining, N.Y.: Catholic Foreign Missionary Society of America, 1906), p. 25.

16. Bernard of Clairvaux, *Doctor Mellifluus*, no. 31.

17. Teresa of Calcutta, p. 139.

18. Augustine, quoted in F.J. Sheed, *Theology for Beginners* (Ann Arbor, Mich.: Servant, 1981), p. 124.

19. Sheed, *Theology for Beginners,* p. 92.

20. Edward Sri, *Dawn of the Messiah: The Coming of Christ in Scripture* (Cincinnati: Servant, 2005), p. 22.

21. Thérèse of Lisieux, quoted in Caster, p. 3.

22. Louis de Montfort, quoted in Ronda de Sola Chervin and Carla Conley, *Catholic Customs and Traditions* (Ann Arbor, Mich.: Servant, 1994), p. 77.

23. Pope John Paul II, *Salvifici Doloris,* Apostolic Letter on the Christian Meaning of Human Suffering (Boston: Pauline, 1984), p. 40.

24. Mike Aquilina, *Angels of God: The Bible, the Church, and the Heavenly Hosts* (Cincinnati: Servant, 2009), p. 72.

25. Gospel of Luke 1:38.

26. Venantius Fortunatus, quoted in Thigpen, p. 143.

27. Bernadette Soubirous, quoted in Lochran, p. 130.

28. Nobisso.

29. Gospel of Luke 1:46–48.

30. John Paul II, *Redemptoris Mater,* Encyclical Letter on the Blessed Virgin Mary in the Life of the Pilgrim Church, no. 36, www.vatican.va.

31. Bonaventure, quoted in Alphonsus de Liguori, *The Glories of Mary,* p. 384.

April

1. Gospel of John 19:27.
2. Augustine of Hippo, quoted in Thigpen, p. 142.
3. Jean du Coeur de Jésus d'Elbée, *I Believe in Love*, Marilyn Teichert with Madeleine Stebbins, trans. (Petersham, Mass.: St. Bede's, 1974), p. 160.
4. Erasmus, *Enchiridion*, quoted in Chapin, *The Book of Catholic Quotations*, p. 101.
5. Gospel of Luke 2:34–35.
6. Pope John Paul II, *Redemptoris Mater*, no. 16.
7. Caster, p. 29.
8. Titles of the Blessed Virgin Mary, *The Mary Page*.
9. Martin Luther, quoted in John Trigilio and Kenneth Brighenti, *Catholicism for Dummies* (Indianapolis: Wiley, 2003), p. 259.
10. Vincent of Lerins, quoted in Thigpen, p. 143.
11. Thomas Merton, *The Seven Storey Mountain* (Orlando, Fla: Harcourt Brace, 1999), p. 144.
12. Johnnette S. Benkovic, *Full of Grace: Women and the Abundant Life* (Cincinnati: Servant, 2004), p. 81.
13. Ambrose, *Ambrose: Selected Works and Letters*, www.ccel.org
14. Just de Bretenières, quoted in James A. Walsh, p. 27.
15. Thomas Merton, *New Seeds of Contemplation*, p. 174.
16. Bernadette Soubirous, quoted in Lochran, p. 51.
17. Lochran, p. 115.
18. Louis de Montfort, quoted in Thigpen, p. 146.
19. Alan Schreck, *Basics of the Faith: A Catholic Catechism* (Ann Arbor, Mich.: Servant, 1987), p. 282.
20. Peter Chrysologus, quoted in Thigpen, p. 143.
21. Bonaventure, adapted from quote in Alphonsus de Liguori, *The Glories of Mary*, p. 42.
22. Pope John Paul II, *Veritatis Splendor*, no. 120, www.vatican.va.
23. F.J. Sheed, *Theology and Sanity* (New York: Sheed & Ward, 1946), p. 273.
24. Josemaría Escrivá, quoted in Mike Aquilina and Regis J. Flaherty, *The How-To Book of Catholic Devotions: Everything You Need to Know But No One Ever Taught You* (Huntington, Ind.: Our Sunday Visitor, 2000), p. 209.
25. Paul Elie, *The Life You Save May Be Your Own: An American Pilgrimage* (New York: Farrar, Straus and Giroux, 2003), p. 439, with quote of Dorothy Day adapted from William D. Miller, *Dorothy Day: A Biography* (San Francisco: Harper Collins, 1984), p. 511.
26. Alan Schreck, *Catholic and Christian*, p. 167.

27. Thomas à Kempis, *The Imitation of Christ,* p. 253, www.ccel.org.

28. Gospel of John 2:3–5.

29. Vatican II, *Lumen Gentium,* Dogmatic Constitution on the Church, no. 65 (Boston: St. Paul, 1964), p. 59.

30. Jacinta Marto, quoted at www.fatimacrusader.com.

May

1. Pope John Paul II, *Rosarium Virginis Mariae,* Apostolic Letter on the Most Holy Rosary, no. 2, www.vatican.va.

2. Excerpt from Gerard Manley Hopkins, "The May Magnificat," quoted at http://campus.udayton.edu.

3. Maximilian Kolbe, quoted in Hardon, "Maximilian Kolbe, Apostle of Mary."

4. Escrivá, *The Way,* no. 498, *The Way/Furrow/The Forge,* p. 122.

5. Francis de Sales, *Treatise on the Love of God,* John Cuthbert Hedley, trans. (Rockford, Ill.: Tan, 1997), bk. 9, chap. 14, p. 400, www.ccel.org.

6. Sheed, *Theology for Beginners,* p. 128.

7. The Blessed Virgin Mary to Bernadette Soubirous, quoted in Lochran, p. 1.

8. Titles of the Blessed Virgin Mary, *The Mary Page.*

9. Pope John Paul II, *Salvifici Doloris,* pp. 40–41.

10. Sheed, *Theology and Sanity,* p. 278.

11. Thérèse of Lisieux, *Her Last Conversations,* p. 161.

12. Théophane Vénard, quoted in James A. Walsh, p. 69.

13. Sister Lucia, quoted in Cardinal Tarcisio Bertone, *The Last Secret of Fatima: My Conversations with Sister Lucia* (New York: Doubleday, 2008), p. 33.

14. Pope John Paul II, homily at Fatima, May 13, 1982, quoted in Schreck, *Catholic and Christian,* p. 201.

15. Anselm of Canterbury, quoted in Thigpen, p. 143.

16. Caster, p. 31.

17. Cardinal Joseph Ratzinger, quoted in Benkovic, pp. 19–20.

18. Ulrich Zwingli, quoted in María Ruiz Scaperlanda, *The Complete Idiot's Guide to Mary of Nazareth* (New York: Penguin, 2006), p. 40.

19. William Bernard Ullathorne, *Letters in the Oscation,* in Chapin, *The Book of Catholic Quotations,* p. 782.

20. C.S. Lewis, in Wayne Martindale and Jerry Root, eds., *The Quotable Lewis* (Wheaton, Ill.: Tyndale House, 1989), p. 570.

21. Cardinal John Henry Newman, quoted in Alfred McBride, "The Maternity of Mary," from *Images of Mary,* www.americancatholic.org.

22. Peter Chrysologus, quoted in Thigpen, p. 143.

23. Sheed, *Theology and Sanity*, p. 275.

24. Ambrose, quoted in Pope Paul VI, *Marialis Cultus*, Apostolic Exhortation for the Right Ordering and Development of Devotion to the Blessed Virgin Mary, February 2, 1974, no. 21, www.vatican.va.

25. Pope Paul VI, *Marialis Cultus*, no. 28, quoting Isaac de Stella, Sermon 51, *In Assumptione B. Mariae*: PL 194, 1863.

26. Bartolo Longo, *The Fifteen Saturdays of the Holy Rosary* (Naples, Italy: Shrine of Pompeii, 1993), p. 29.

27. McBride, "The Maternity of Mary."

28. Scott Hahn, *Hail, Holy Queen*, p. 91.

29. Bernard of Clairvaux, quoted in Thigpen, p. 143.

30. Louis de Montfort, *True Devotion to Mary*, no. 24, available at www.ewtn.com.

31. Gospel of Luke 1:42.

June

1. Alphonsus de Liguori, *The Glories of Mary*, p. 27.

2. Day, "About Mary," in *Selected Writings*, p. 159.

3. Bernadette Soubirous, quoted in Lochran, p. 26.

4. Sheed, *Theology for Beginners*, p. 128.

5. Teresa Benedicta of the Cross, quoted in Benkovic, p. 22.

6. Bernard of Clairvaux, quoted in Thigpen, p.144.

7. Mike Aquilina, *Love in the Little Things: Tales of Family Life* (Cincinnati: Servant, 2007), p. 113.

8. Excerpt from Hymn to Mary, quoted in Lochran, p. 38.

9. Adrienne von Speyr, quoted in Scaperlanda, p. 247.

10. Elie, pp. 178–179.

11. Kimberly Hahn, *Graced and Gifted: Biblical Wisdom for the Homemaker's Heart* (Cincinnati: Servant, 2008), p. 127.

12. Longo, *The Fifteen Saturdays*, p. 34.

13. Henri Rondet, "Mary in the Plan of God," *The Marian Era*, vol. 9, p. 72.

14. Alice von Hildebrand, *The Privilege of Being a Woman* (Ann Arbor, Mich.: Sapientia, 2005), p. 83.

15. Titles of the Blessed Virgin Mary, *The Mary Page*.

16. Lawrence G. Lovasik, *A Novena of Holy Communions* (Rockford, Ill.: Tan, 1995), p. 8.

17. Pope John Paul II, *Redemptoris Mater*, no. 46.

18. Excerpt from Gerard Manley Hopkins, "The Blessed Virgin Compared to the Air We Breathe," Project Gutenberg, www.gutenberg.org.
19. Edith Stein, *Essays on Woman,* vol. 2, *The Collected Works of Edith Stein* (Washington, D.C.: ICS, 1987), p. 52.
20. De Montfort, *True Devotion to Mary,* no. 27.
21. Augustine, *On Christian Doctrine,* bk. 1, chap. 14, no. 13, www.ccel.org.
22. Pope Pius XII, quoted in Mark Miravalle, *Mary: Coredemptrix, Mediatrix, Advocate* (Santa Barbara, Calif.: Queenship, 1993), p. 19.
23. Longo, *The Fifteen Saturdays,* p. 101.
24. Jean-Pierre de Caussade, *Abandonment to Divine Providence,* bk. 1, chap. 1, sect. 1, www.ccel.org.
25. Francis de Sales, *Introduction to the Devout Life,* chap. 16, www.ccel.org.
26. Henry Suso, *A Little Book of Eternal Wisdom,* pt. 1, chap. 17, www.ccel.org.
27. Bernard of Clairvaux, quoted in Alphonsus de Liguori, *The Glories of Mary,* p. 16.
28. Gospel of Luke 2:50–51.
29. Sri, *Dawn of the Messiah,* pp. 104–105.
30. Bonaventure, quoted in Alphonsus de Liguori, *The Glories of Mary,* p. 6.

July

1. Teresa of Avila, *Life of St. Teresa of Jesus of the Order of Our Lady of Carmel,* available at: http://www.ccel.org/ccel/teresa/life.viii.ii.html.
2. "August 14, Saint Maximilian Kolbe," Saint of the Day, www.american-catholic.org.
3. Bernadette Soubirous, quoted in Lochran, p. 126.
4. Ronald Knox, *A Retreat for Lay People* (New York: Sheed and Ward, 1955), pp. 252–253.
5. De Caussade, bk. 1, chap. 1, sect. 2.
6. Titles of the Blessed Virgin Mary, *The Mary Page.*
7. Francis of Assisi, quoted in Thigpen, p. 144.
8. *Lumen Gentium,* no. 56, www.vatican.va.
9. Longo, *The Fifteen Saturdays,* p. 149.
10. Aquilina, *Love in the Little Things,* p. 17.
11. Peter Damian, *De Nativ. S.* 1, quoted at www.catholictreasury.info.
12. Bernard, quoted in Alphonsus de Liguori, *The Glories of Mary,* p. 16.
13. Abbot William, quoted in Alphonsus de Liguori, *The Glories of Mary,* p. 23.
14. John Chrysostom, quoted in Sheed, *Theology for Beginners,* p. 129.
15. Aloysius Novarinus, quoted in Alphonsus de Liguori, *The Glories of Mary,* p. 26.

16. Chaplet of Our Lady, Star of the Sea, *The Mary Page.*

17. Bernadette Soubirous, quoted in Lochran, p. 130.

18. *Catechism of the Catholic Church*, #489, p. 123, quoting *Lumen Gentium*, no. 55.

19. Sri, *Dawn of the Messiah*, p. 42.

20. Richard of St. Lawrence, quoted in Alphonsus de Liguori, *The Glories of Mary*, p. 35.

21. Pope Benedict XVI, General Audience, August 12, 2009, www.vatican.va.

22. Houselander, "A Secret Form of Virgin Emptiness," in Wright, p. 106.

23. Gospel of John 19:25.

24. Alphonsus de Liguori, *The Glories of Mary*, p. 45.

25. Schreck, *Basics of the Faith*, p. 286.

26. Pope John Paul II, *Redemptoris Mater*, no. 21.

27. Bonaventure, quoted in Thigpen, p. 144.

28. Excerpt from Maximilian Kolbe, Prayer of Total Consecration, referring to Genesis 3:15 and a prayer of priests, www.consecration.com.

29. Pope John Paul II, *Veritatis Splendor*, no. 120.

30. Bonaventure, quoted in Alphonsus de Liguori, *The Glories of Mary*, p. 52.

31. Bernard of Clairvaux, The Memorare, adapted from www.ewtn.com.

August

1. Pope John Paul II, *Redemptoris Mater*, no. 46.

2. Sheed, *Theology for Beginners*, p. 133.

3. Thomas Aquinas, quoted in Thigpen, p. 144.

4. Graham Greene, quoted in Scaperlanda, p. 317.

5. Longo, *The Fifteen Saturdays*, p. 338.

6. Bernadette Soubirous, quoted in Lochran, p. 130.

7. Benkovic, pp. 200–201.

8. Bernard, quoted at www.catholictreasury.info.

9. Dorothy Day, quoted in John Samaha, "Dorothy Day," http://campus.udayton.edu.

10. Albert the Great, quoted in Alphonsus de Liguori, *The Glories of Mary*, p. 35.

11. The Blessed Virgin to Bernadette Soubirous, quoted in Lochran, p. 2.

12. *Lumen Gentium,* no. 60.

13. Thomas Aquinas, quoted in Thigpen, p. 144.

14. Schreck, *Catholic and Christian*, p. 194.

15. Bernard of Clairvaux, quoted in Thigpen, p. 146.

16. Robert Bellarmine, quoted in Thigpen, p. 147.

17. Thomas Merton, *New Seeds of Contemplation,* p. 173.

18. Weigel, p. 57.

19. Pope Benedict XVI, homily, "The Feast of the Assumption, a Day of Joy," August 16, 2005, quoted at www.crossroadsinitiative.com.

20. Scott Hahn, *A Father Who Keeps His Promises: God's Covenant Love in Scripture* (Ann Arbor, Mich.: Servant, 1998), p. 73.

21. Titles of the Blessed Virgin Mary, *The Mary Page.*

22. John Henry Newman, quoted in Thigpen, p. 148.

23. Revelation 12:1.

24. De Caussade, bk. 1, chap. 2, sect. 2.

25. Thomas Aquinas, quoted in Thigpen, p. 144.

26. Thérèse of Lisieux, *The Story of a Soul,* chap. 4, www.ccel.org.

27. John Henry Newman, A Short Service for Rosary Sunday, *Meditations and Devotions,* www.newmanreader.org.

28. Bridget of Sweden, quoted in Thigpen, p. 144.

29. Caster, p. 31.

30. Francis de Sales, quoted in Thigpen, p. 244.

31. Bonaventure, quoted in Alphonsus de Liguori, *The Glories of Mary,* p. 6.

September

1. Shea, *By What Authority?* pp. 146–147.

2. Maximilian Kolbe, "Mary Personifies Man's Perfect Union With God," *Miles Immaculatae,* January 1938, www.consecration.com.

3. Bernadette Soubirous, quoted in Lochran, p. 130.

4. Bernardine of Siena, quoted in Thigpen, p. 145.

5. Pope Paul VI, *Marialis Cultus,* no. 57.

6. Escrivá, *The Way,* no. 499, *The Way/Furrow/The Forge,* p. 122.

7. Sheed, *Theology for Beginners,* pp. 129–130.

8. Andrew of Crete, quoted in Thigpen, p. 147.

9. Martin Luther, Sermon, "On the Day of the Conception of the Mother of God," 1527, quoted in Dave Armstrong, "Martin Luther's Devotion to Mary," www.catholicculture.org.

10. Stein, *Essays on Woman,* p. 234.

11. John Vianney, quoted in Thigpen, p. 145.

12. Mark Shea, *Myths and Ancient Truth,* vol. 1, *Mary, Mother of the Son* (San Diego: Catholic Answers, 2009), p. 145.

13. Pope John Paul II, *Veritatis Splendor,* no. 120.

14. Louis de Montfort, quoted in Thigpen, p. 145.

15. Lawrence Justinian, quoted in Alphonsus de Liguori, *The Glories of Mary*, p. 384.

16. Titles of the Blessed Virgin Mary, *The Mary Page*.

17. Lewis, *Miracles*, p. 138.

18. Kerry Crawford, *Lourdes Today: A Pilgrimage to Mary's Grotto* (Cincinnati: Servant, 2008), p. 91.

19. Pope John Paul II, *Ordinatio Sacerdotalis*, Apostolic Letter on Reserving Priestly Ordination to Men, no. 3, www.vatican.va.

20. John of Damascus, quoted in Thigpen, p. 147.

21. Francis de Sales, *Introduction to the Devout Life*, chap. 18.

22. Von Hildebrand, p. 104.

23. Sri, *Dawn of the Messiah*, p. 32.

24. Thomas Aquinas, *Summa Theologica*, 3, 29, I, quoted in Chapin, *The Book of Catholic Quotations*, p. 82.

25. Hilaire Belloc, *The Path to Rome*, www.gutenberg.org.

26. John of Damascus, *Exposition of the Orthodox Faith*, 4, 16, quoted in Chapin, *The Book of Catholic Quotations*, p. 82.

27. Englebert, p. 243.

28. Teresa of Calcutta, *Thirsting for God*, pp. 157–158.

29. Thomas Aquinas, *Summa Theologica*, 3, 26, I, quoted in Chapin, *The Book of Catholic Quotations*, p. 91.

30. Leo Joseph Suenens, *Mary the Mother of God* (New York: Hawthorn, n.d.), p. 10, quoted in William K. McDonough, *The Divine Family: The Trinity and Our Life in God* (Cincinnati: Servant, 2005), p. 128.

October

1. Acts 1:14.

2. Thérèse of Liseux, *Story of a Soul*, chap. 13, www.ccel.org.

3. John Henry Newman, quoted in Thigpen, p. 146.

4. Thomas Merton, *No Man Is an Island* (New York: Harcourt Brace, 1983), p. 209.

5. Sheed, *Theology for Beginners*, p. 132.

6. Sheed, *Theology for Beginners*, p. 132.

7. Lochran, p. 118.

8. Lochran, p. 120.

9. Thomas Merton, "Our Lady of Cobre," in Thomas P. McDonnell, ed., *A Thomas Merton Reader* (New York: Image, 1989), p. 79.

10. Francis of Assisi, excerpt from "Salutation to the Blessed Virgin Mary," from *The Catholic Devotional* (Oakdale, Minn.: Apostolic, 1999), p. 16.

11. Bartolo Longo, quoted in Pope John Paul II, *Rosarium Virginis Mariae*, no. 43.

12. Maximilian Kolbe, "Mary Personifies Man's Perfect Union With God."

13. Pope John Paul II, Homily, Lourdes, August 15, 2004, no. 5, quoted in Crawford, p. 95.

14. Ullathorne, *Letters in the Oscation*, quoted in Chapin, *The Book of Catholic Quotations*, p. 782.

15. John of Damascus, quoted in Thigpen, p. 147.

16. Pope John Paul II, *Rosarium Virginis Mariae*, no. 3.

17. Pope John Paul II, *Rosarium Virginis Mariae*, no. 10.

18. Alphonsus de Liguori, *The Glories of Mary*, p. 37.

19. Caster, p. 99.

20. Pope John Paul II, *Redemptoris Mater*, no. 17.

21. Timothy M. Dolan, *To Whom Shall We Go? Lessons from the Apostle Peter* (Huntington, Ind.: Our Sunday Visitor, 2008), p. 99.

22. Bartolo Longo, quoted in Ann M. Brown, *Apostle of the Rosary: Blessed Bartolo Longo* (New Hope, Ky.: New Hope, 2004), p. 53.

23. De Montfort, *True Devotion to Mary*, no. 53.

24. Bernadette Soubirous, quoted in Lochran, p. 130.

25. Titles of the Blessed Virgin Mary, *The Mary Page*.

26. D'Elbée, p. 160.

27. Abram Ryan, "My Beads," Project Gutenberg, www.gutenberg.org.

28. Ambrose, "The Mirror of Our Lady," in John Chapin, *A Treasury of Catholic Reading* (New York: Farrar, Straus and Cudahy, 1957), p. 39.

29. Bernard of Clairvaux, quoted in Thigpen, p. 147.

30. Peter John Cameron, *The Classics of Catholic Spirituality* (Staten Island, N.Y.: Alba House, 1996), p. 98.

31. Thomas Aquinas, quoted in Alphonsus de Liguori, *The Glories of Mary*, pp. 617–618.

November

1. Gospel of Matthew 13:53–55.

2. Richard John Neuhaus, *Death on a Friday Afternoon: Meditations on the Last Words of Jesus on the Cross* (New York: Basic, 2000), p. 73.

3. Francis de Sales, *Introduction to the Devout Life*, chap. 17.

4. Marcel Schlewer, *All My People: Why She Spoke, Why She Wept at La Salette*, James P. O'Reilly, trans. (Enfield, N.H.: Grassroots, 1998), pp. 131, 132, 133.

5. Byzantine Liturgy, Troparian, Feast of the Dormition, August 15, quoted in *Catechism of the Catholic Church*, no. 966, p. 252.

6. Longo, *The Fifteen Saturdays*, pp. 336–337.

7. Michael Scanlan, *The Holy Spirit: Holy Desire* (Steubenville, Ohio: Franciscan University Press, 1998), pp. 32–33.

8. Sheed, *Theology for Beginners*, pp. 132–133.

9. Pope Pius IX, *Ubi Primum*, Encyclical on the Immaculate Conception, February 2, 1849, no. 5, www.ewtn.com.

10. Thomas Merton, excerpt from "Canticle for the Blessed Virgin," http://campus.udayton.edu.

11. Bonaventure, quoted in Thigpen, p. 147.

12. Titles of the Blessed Virgin Mary, *The Mary Page*.

13. John Henry Newman, *Meditations and Devotions*, quoted in Chapin, *The Book of Catholic Quotations*, p. 97.

14. De Montfort, *True Devotion to Mary*, no. 85.

15. National Conference of Catholic Bishops, Behold Your Mother, Woman of Faith: A Pastoral Letter on the Blessed Virgin Mary (Washington, D.C.: Publications Office USCC, 1973), p. 27.

16. Irenaeus of Lyons, *Against Heresies*, bk. 3, 22, 4, quoted in Schreck, *Catholic and Christian*, p. 168.

17. Scott Hahn, *A Father Who Keeps His Promises*, p. 243.

18. Alban Goodier, *Inner Life of the Catholic*, quoted in Chapin, *The Book of Catholic Quotations*, p. 102.

19. Gerard Manley Hopkins, excerpt from "The Blessed Virgin Compared to the Air We Breathe," www.gutenberg.org.

20. *Lumen Gentium*, no. 62, quoted in Schreck, *Basics of the Faith*, p. 286.

21. Houselander, "A Secret Form of Virgin Emptiness," in Wright, p. 107.

22. D'Elbée, p. 163.

23. Lochran, p. 81.

24. Pope Benedict XVI, *Deus Caritas Est*, Encyclical Letter on Christian Love, no. 42, December 25, 2005, www.vatican.va, and quoted in Crawford, pp. 108–109.

25. Andrew Apostoli, Walk *Humbly With Your God: Simple Steps to a Virtuous Life* (Cincinnati: Servant, 2006), p. 172.

26. De Montfort, *True Devotion to Mary*, no. 36.

27. Just de Bretenières, quoted in James A. Walsh, p. 27.

28. Edith Stein, *Essays on Woman*, p. 267.

29. Escrivá, *The Way*, no. 508, *The Way/Furrow/The Forge*, p. 124.

30. North American Lourdes Volunteer sign, posted at a campus in Austria, quoted in Crawford, p. 67.

December

1. Newman, *Meditations and Devotions*, p. 261, www.newmanreader.org.
2. Gospel of Matthew 1:23.
3. National Conference of Catholic Bishops, *Mary in the Church: A Selection of Teaching Documents,* no. 85, p. 32.
4. Pope John Paul II, Papal Address, "Mary's Motherhood Acquired at the Foot of the Cross," May 11, 1983, quoted in Miravalle, p. 46.
5. Ephrem of Syria, quoted in Mike Aquilina, *The Fathers of the Church: An Introduction to the First Christian Teachers* (Huntington, Ind.: Our Sunday Visitor, 2006), p. 142.
6. Antonius, quoted at catholictreasury.info.
7. Sheed, *Theology for Beginners*, p. 129.
8. Aquilina, *Angels of God,* p. 72.
9. Maximilian Kolbe, "Mary Personifies Man's Perfect Union With God."
10. Bernard of Clairvaux, adapted from *Doctor Mellifluus,* no. 31.
11. John Henry Newman, quoted in Thigpen, p. 146.
12. Our Lady, quoted in Virgilio Elizondo and friends, *A Retreat With Our Lady of Guadalupe and Juan Diego: Heeding the Call* (Cincinnati: St. Anthony Messenger Press, 1998), p. 13.
13. Titus Brandsma, *Ejercicios,* p. 5, quoted in *Redemptus,* Maria Valabek, ed., *Essays on Titus Brandsma* (Rome: Carmel in the World Paperbacks, 1985), p. 201.
14. John of the Cross, *Del Verbo Divino,* in Kieran Kavanaugh and Otilio Rodriguez, trans., *Collected Works of St. John of the Cross* (Washington, D.C.: ICS, 1979), p. 737.
15. De Montfort, *True Devotion to Mary,* no. 107.
16. John Henry Newman, *Meditations and Devotions,* p. 261, www.newmanreader.org.
17. Titles of the Blessed Virgin Mary, *The Mary Page.*
18. G.K. Chesterton, *The Everlasting Man* (San Francisco: Ignatius, 1993), p. 184.
19. St. Bernard of Clairvaux, adapted from quote in Alphonsus de Liguori, *The Glories of Mary,* pp. 248–249.
20. Sheed, *Theology for Beginners,* p. 127.
21. Longo, *Fifteen Saturdays,* pp. 85–86.
22. Chesterton, *The Everlasting Man,* p. 171.
23. John Donne, excerpt from "Nativity," quoted at http://campus.udayton.edu
24. G.K. Chesterton, "The House of Christmas," www.gutenberg.org.
25. *Christian Prayer: The Liturgy of the Hours,* Christmas, Antiphon at Second Vespers, (New York: Catholic Book Publishing, 1976), p. 150.
26. *Byzantine Menaea,* Feast of the Nativity, Canon at Matins, Ninth Ode, quoted in Chapin, *The Book of Catholic Quotations,* p. 167.
27. Catherine Labouré, quoted in Englebert, p. 126.

28. Sigrid Unset, "Christmas and Epiphany," quoted in Chapin, *A Treasury of Catholic Reading,* p. 45.

29. Ephrem the Syrian, quoted in Thigpen, p. 142.

30. Teresa of Calcutta, quoted in Scaperlanda, p. 13.

31. Benedict XVI, "The Feast of the Assumption, a Day of Joy."

ABOUT THE AUTHOR

KAREN EDMISTEN is the author of *The Rosary: Keeping Company with Jesus and Mary*. A popular blogger whose work has appeared in numerous Catholic magazines, she lives with her husband and daughters in the Midwest. Find her online at www.karenedmisten.com.